T0324132

ACCOMPANIED VOICES

ACCOMPANIED VOICES

POETS ON COMPOSERS FROM THOMAS TALLIS TO ARVO PÄRT

selected by John Greening

THE BOYDELL PRESS

First published 2015
The Boydell Press, Woodbridge

ISBN 978-1-78327-015-6

The Boydell Press is an imprint of Boydell & Brewer Ltd
PO Box 9, Woodbridge, Suffolk IP12 3DF, UK
and of Boydell & Brewer Inc.
668 Mt Hope Avenue, Rochester, NY 14620–2731, USA
website: www.boydellandbrewer.com

A CIP catalogue record for this book is available
from the British Library

The publisher has no responsibility for the continued existence or
accuracy of URLs for external or third-party internet websites referred
to in this book, and does not guarantee that any content on such
websites is, or will remain, accurate or appropriate

This publication is printed on acid-free paper

CONTENTS

Music

No, Pater, no:
All art does not aspire to its condition.
Haydn, Mozart, Schubert, Mahler, Britten
Speak what we cannot speak, beyond the sayable,
Translate the universe into the playable.
Our lesser arts must learn how to be humble.
And words? Just listen to them stumble.

NEIL POWELL

INTRODUCTION

Poets have been inspired by music for centuries, but with the arrival of recordings and the possibility of repeated listening there was an extraordinary upsurge in poems about specific pieces and named composers. There followed a century of responses, fascinating to the poetry lover, delightful to the music lover, and irresistible to those who are both. In putting together *Accompanied Voices*, I have drawn chiefly on this hoard of largely overlooked material – often by major poets. The result is, I believe, a unique book. Not only is it an anthology of some of the most memorable and accessible international writing about classical music, and a moving commentary by one set of practising artists on the work of another; it is also something of a guide in verse (the language which comes closest to music itself) to the great composers of the past five hundred years. My hope is that the reader might find the same pleasure in turning these pages that they would find in putting on a CD and listening.

When there is any news coverage at all of classical music, it tends to be about scandals, ageing audiences or funding cuts. Meanwhile, I suspect that things are much as they ever were: there are still young people out there being swept away by their first experience of *The Rite of Spring*, just as there are grey heads puzzling over a new Maxwell Davies *Naxos Quartet*. Or perhaps it is the other way round. The late Robert Tear, who was a poet as well as a wonderful tenor, even wrote in the *Guardian* shortly before he died that he would like to let music lie fallow, to 'give audiences time to really want to hear music again. Having been starved of it for five years, they would demand it.' While less confident than Tear, I do believe that music is not only the food of love but the food of life itself. It is this conviction – and, in my case certainly, a spirit of envious rivalry – that has moved so many poets to write about it. Everybody can think of a quotation about music in the abstract, be it from Orsino's opening lines to *Twelfth Night* or Shelley's 'Music, when soft voices die …', but there are also hundreds about particular pieces of music by particular composers heard in particular places. Mozart in Kosovo, Bach in Nazi Germany, Richard Strauss in the trenches. These are poems which acknowledge music as one of the keys to survival.

It is surprising how few poems about identifiable composers were in fact written before the First World War. Anthologies of music poetry have tended to rely on the more abstract responses of famous (out of copyright) authors and the result can be a rather over-rarefied experience, as in Duncan and August MacDougall's *The Bond of*

Music (London, 1907) or Douglas Brooks-Davies's *What Sweeter Music* (London, 1999). One sonnet 'To Music' or to a skylark or nightingale is much like another. John Bishop's *Music and Sweet Poetry* (London, 1968) largely avoided this problem by using eyes as well as ears, looking to the earth as well as to the sky, and by including some of the poems of place and personality beginning to appear in the 1960s. Readers familiar with Bishop's lovely book will recognise several old friends here. More recently, two American publications, *The Music Lover's Anthology of Poetry* (New York, 2007) and *Music's Spell* (New York, 2009), took a similar thematic approach.

However, in editing this rather differently accented new anthology, I made two decisions: first, not to include a poem just because it is the standard piece on that composer – so, no Hopkins on Purcell or Brooke on Wagner or Spender on Beethoven – and secondly, bearing in mind Peter Porter's observation that 'music and literature are bound by time, which the plastic arts are not', to present the poems chronologically, by composer. My aim was to provide a tour of Western Music in the company of a hundred or so interesting guides – not necessarily guides who are experts, but who are all virtuosi in language and able to make their insights entertaining. In turn, they would represent a range of poetic styles and give some impression of the way, just as poetry has frequently inspired composers, compositions have very often brought out the best in poets.

Some have done so by imagining themselves into the period when the music was written; some have remained very much in their own time. There are those for whom the experience is intensely spiritual (nothing from *Four Quartets* quite fitted here, yet it is worth remembering that T. S. Eliot modelled them on late Beethoven), those for whom it is sensual, intellectual, amused, bewildered or simply part of a historical narrative. There are highly sophisticated responses complete with musical terminology, and there are those of the musical innocent. A few of the poets here studied music (Marcia Menter, Joanna Boulter), were born into it (Kevin Crossley-Holland's father was a composer), have published books on it (David Holbrook, Neil Powell, Andrew Motion), had active careers in it (Gwen Harwood, Humphrey Clucas, Maurice Lindsay, Gregory Warren Wilson, Fiona Sampson) or (like Anne Stevenson and Carol Rumens) originally hoped to. One or two poets, such as Alfred Corn and Dana Gioia, have followed Ezra Pound's example and written music themselves. Many sing or play an instrument – usually the piano, but there are fiddlers three at least, and clarinettists enough to make a poets' ensemble. In Michael Donaghy's case it was the tin whistle, for he was a successful folk musician as well as a spellbinding poetry performer who, like a classical virtuoso, had everything by heart. Composers' partners can bring heart of a different kind, and while there is no Alice Elgar, I am very pleased to feature some Ursula Vaughan Williams. Then there is artistic partnership: there are several librettists among the featured poets, from John Dryden to

David Harsent. At least two of the contributors offer words set to the rhythms of a certain composition – Hardy to Mozart, Ronald Duncan to Schubert. One name here – Ivor Gurney's – will chime with poetry lovers and music lovers, as he was wooed by both of the blest Sirens; and another, Dermot O'Byrne, may be better known as the twilit alter ego of Sir Arnold Bax, Master of the King's (and Queen's) Musick. A more recent holder of the same post, Peter Maxwell Davies, who has so often set George Mackay Brown, is himself 'set' by the Orkney poet to commemorate his sixtieth birthday. Many more of the poets approach their subject as simply as music lovers or responsive human beings moved to the quick by what they have heard or heard about. Invariably, they consider the composers fellow artists and see parallels between the creative processes.

Before the appearance of discs the main focus for poets writing about classical music was the piano – although that fascination with the intimacy of hands at a keyboard has never gone away. Siegfried Sassoon, while keeping up as a pianist and concert-goer, is among the earliest to make recorded music one of his preoccupations. Others, like Roy Fuller and Peter Porter, soon followed. The very act of putting on a record generated a new world of symbolism: the needle in the groove, the ghostly repeatability ... Some, of course, were suspicious. The musicologist Hans Keller used to argue that recorded music meant we could forever put off having to concentrate. The conductor Antal Dorati reminded us that a fixed smile can become a grimace. But in one form or another the 'gramophone' was here to stay: a rather inviting rhyme word for poets, who nowadays are stuck with 'CD player', 'iPod' or 'download', although 'streaming' has a certain promise. That awed celebration of abundance, however, has turned to something more like nausea by the time we find ourselves 'In the CD Shop' with William Scammell:

> Rack upon rack of music
> – the visceral art –
> from Hildegard of Bingen
> to Arvo Pärt.
>
> You would need several lifetimes,
> each one profane
> just to slit open
> the clear cellophane ...

Scammell might have bumped into any number of poets in that (*o rare!*) CD shop, but most probably it would have been Peter Porter, whose record collection was legendary. Yet many of the contemporary poems are responses to live concerts or private performances. A number, of course, depend – as does music itself – on memory, taking a melody as the starting point for a journey. There are a good few elegies. Often the music is associated with a location. The composer's life is an inevitable source and there are lively anecdotes and vivid snapshots (Ezra Pound watching Stravinsky's funeral, Mozart playing billiards), but there are poems which are not 'about' a particular composer at all; rather, they are 'about' the poet. This is one reason why I have given the collection the title 'Accompanied Voices'. Just as the performers are equal partners in a sonata, so are poet and composer here. That the poets are overwhelmingly of our time, many still alive and writing, makes the collaboration all the more compelling.

There is work which had to be dropped because permission could not be obtained. Yet there have been delightful and generous donations of poems, in many cases previously unpublished, by some of the most distinguished writers of our time. For other work there was simply no room: Anthony Hecht's extended homage to Haydn, 'A Love for Four Voices'; or either of two book-length sequences on Shostakovich, from which I only offer what Donald Tovey called 'bleeding chunks' (he was thinking of excerpts from Wagner operas), by Joanna Boulter and Gareth Reeves. The latter, incidentally, represents one of two father/son combinations here as we also have James Reeves, as well as Roy and John Fuller. Other poems didn't fit for aesthetic reasons. How tempting, for example, to have begun in the twelfth century with Hildegard herself and Selima Hill's wickedly surreal miniature, 'Portrait of My Lover as Hildegard of Bingen':

> O take yourself to Bingen
> and a cell
> with a narrow bed
> and spectacular views of the sea
> and a constant supply
> of uplifting musical instruments
> shaped like intestines
> made of beaten gold.

But Tallis's forty-part motet proved the more seductive opening, not least because of a wonderful interconnectedness: Byrd elegises Tallis; short-lived Sidney Keyes writes in the voice of the aged Byrd; Hal Summers sets his own Byrd poem during the war which killed Keyes. Such links and coincidences continue throughout the book. While it is no surprise to find several writers reaching for the 'Music of the Spheres', who would have guessed that so many would be drawn to the death of Anton Webern? And how delightful to find the chance juxtaposition of two very local English poets, Nicholson and Causley, each presenting a formal tribute, one to Grieg, one to Fauré. Not infrequently, the music that prompts a poem was itself inspired by another poem. So, George Meredith writes a poem about a lark ascending, Vaughan Williams responds, and his work becomes a favourite of today's poets. Poetry, after all, used to lead the other arts. There is no recent equivalent to the effect of Byron or Scott, although Hardy and Whitman have been very influential.

Sometimes we lost major poems because they were on very minor composers: John Milton on Lawes, Browning on Galuppi, W. S. Graham on Quantz are, however, readily available in other anthologies. We do have Peter Warlock and Amy Beach and other unexpected figures to compensate. While fully aware that any discussion of a canon is controversial, and noting too a certain bias towards English composers, I have tried (never compromising on poetic quality) to represent the best-known names in the concert repertoire, although in some cases the choice was limited and I did not want to replicate Dannie and Joan Abse's landmark anthology, *The Music Lover's Literary Companion* (London, 1988) by resorting to prose, nor to make the task unmanageable by considering translations. It has to be said that even before he won the Nobel Prize I was very tempted to dip into the 'Haydnpockets' of Tomas Tranströmer, to place alongside the poems here by his translator, Robin Fulton Macpherson.

If a decision had to be made, however, I dropped any poem which was too similar in some respect to another poem, unless that very similarity was illuminating. I intended *Accompanied Voices* to have the virtues of a well-constructed piece of music: variety of tone and colour. I hoped it would be enjoyable even to those unfamiliar with the music. Consequently, there may be absent friends – among the actual composers represented, too. Fewer poets writing in English seem to have been drawn to Spain or Latin America; and it was a long while before good poems turned up on Czech composers, on Prokofiev and other Russians, or on Bruckner and Berlioz – although these last two do have top billing in Dana Gioia's tour de force, 'Lives of the Great Composers' (page xix), which is a witty commentary on biography as well as music, and even emulates a musical form with its fugal repetitions. It sets the tone for the entire anthology. With Bach, Mozart, Beethoven, Schubert, and indeed with Shostakovich and Britten, there was the opposite problem: I could have doubled the numbers of poems included and I regret particularly the loss of those by poets who write so well and so regularly on music. John Heath-Stubbs and Charles Tomlinson might have stocked this volume between them – the one blind, the other a painter, interestingly.

There are also – not too controversially, I hope – some of my own poems. My involvement in music is chiefly as a passionate listener, although I have been known to scrape the violin and worked for a while as Hans Keller's clerk in his last year as head of Radio 3's New Music department. Craig Raine's elegy for Hans, in which he writes how we 'learn that a life can come to an end/like a Haydn quartet, without a repeat', was one of many fine poems I had to persuade myself to omit from *Accompanied Voices*. But Hans knew that I wrote poetry (because, as I explained, I could not compose music) and he was happy to let me scribble away in my office between taking cups of coffee to Edmund Rubbra or Susan Bradshaw or Richard Arnell, the 'reading panel' for unsolicited scores. Music has been central to my own writing ever since, and I shall never forget hearing the Dunedin Consort sing my words in the Wigmore Hall; or listening to Roderick Williams before I read war poetry at Vaughan Williams's house, Leith Hill Place. Although my daughters laugh at the 'geekishness' that still makes me play the game of guessing the composer when we turn on the radio, I am delighted that both have turned out to be equally passionate about classical music and are accomplished performers. Being brought up in a house where there is always something blaring could so easily have alienated them. That it did not gives me hope for the future of music.

JOHN GREENING

Lives of the Great Composers

Herr Bruckner often wandered into church
to join the mourners at a funeral.
The relatives of Berlioz were horrified.
'Such harmony,' quoth Shakespeare, 'is in
immortal souls … We cannot hear it.' But
the radio is playing, and outside
rain splashes to the pavement. Now and then
the broadcast fails. On nights like these Schumann
would watch the lightning streak his windowpanes.

Outside the rain is falling on the pavement.
A scrap of paper tumbles down the street.
On rainy evenings Schumann jotted down
his melodies on windowpanes. 'Such harmony!
We cannot hear it.' The radio goes off and on.
At the rehearsal Gustav Holst exclaimed,
'I'm sick of music, especially my own!'
The relatives of Berlioz were horrified.
Haydn's wife used music to line pastry pans.

On rainy nights the ghost of Mendelssohn
brought melodies for Schumann to compose.
'Such harmony is in immortal souls …
We cannot hear it.' One could suppose
Herr Bruckner would have smiled. At Tergensee
the peasants stood to hear young Paganini play,
but here there's lightning and the thunder rolls.
The radio goes off and on. The rain
falls to the pavement like applause.

A scrap of paper tumbles down the street.
On rainy evenings Schumann would look out
and scribble on the windows of his cell.
'Such harmony.' Cars splash out in the rain.
The relatives of Berlioz were horrified
to see the horses break from the cortege
and gallop with his casket to the grave.
Liszt wept to hear young Paganini play.
Haydn's wife used music to line pastry pans.

DANA GIOIA

THOMAS TALLIS (1505–85)

Spem in Alium

I have placed my hope in no other god but thee,
Transfiguring spirit of poetry,
And as the levels of the landscape rise
In roofline, tree and hill before my eyes,
Until the clouds themselves are earthed in light,
Their changes show the world is not complete
And never will be, as we read its book,
Transfiguration glancing with each look,
Whenever light (changing itself) descries
Another variation for the eyes,
All climbing like a counterpoint of voices,
And sight aware of what, unsighted, stays
Hidden behind a foreground and a meaning
Which cannot be restricted to the thing
Shorn of the spaces that surround its being.
Tallis, you tell the poet what is here
As if that arch of song which throngs the ear,
Shaping not only the invisible,
Rang like the currency of daylight, full
Of the nearby and the answering distances,
Outward and far to where the horizon lies:
And in the altered light there, you can weigh
The pull of the planet travelling its sky,
And one more journey to another day
Complete, and waiting on a dawn unseen,
Unhurriedly to let the changes re-begin.

CHARLES TOMLINSON

Ye Sacred Muses

Ye sacred Muses, race of Jove,
Whom Music's love delighteth,
Come down from crystal heavens above
To earth where Sorrow dwelleth
In mourning weeds, with tears in eyes.
Tallis is dead, and Music dies.

ANONYMOUS, 17th CENTURY, *set by William Byrd.*

WILLIAM BYRD (?1543–1623)

William Byrd

I have come very far, Lord. In my time
Men's mouths have been shut up, the gabble and whine
Of shot has drowned the singing. You will pardon
My praise that rises only from a book –
(How long shall that book be hidden
Under a scarecrow gown, under evil writings?)
And you will pardon the tricks, the secret rooms,
The boarded windows, your house again a stall.
These things have made my house of praise more holy.
And so I try to remember how it was
When lovers sang like finches and the Word
Was music.
                Lord, I am no coward,
But an old man remembering the candle-flames
Reflected in the scroll-work, frozen trees
Praying for Advent, the willow cut at Easter.
The quires are dumb. My spirit sings in silence.
You will appoint the day of my arising.

November 1942

SIDNEY KEYES

William Byrd's Virginal Music from My Ladye Nevells Booke (1591)

It is music that pervades the room
like the scent of roses.

Did you intend your notes
to be so intimate?

How skilfully they lift the veil
of your lady's chamber.

So much so, we listen
not entirely to pavane and galliard

but see eyes drawn to eyes
and hands that gently touch

until all that each heart desires
is found in modest harmony.

EDWARD STOREY

JOHN DOWLAND (?1563–1626)

O Dowland, Old John Dowland

O Dowland, old John Dowland, make a tune for this,
Two lovers married, like two turtle-doves,
Whose mutual eyes no curtain knew nor shade their kiss
And fruitful with a child their holiday loves.

Set that to harmony and then beside it set
Heaven steeled with armament and nations bent
On conquest and resistance, the unavoided net
Of time still drawn in moment by moment.

Is there for such sorrow and love, Dowland, a tune
In your book? Heavy is it for lute to lift?
Yet must we make our poem of it and on the dune
Of this century scatter our sea-thrift.

HAL SUMMERS

Mrs John Dowland

Do they ask after me
the foreign musicians,
when you play the galliard
for two upon one lute?

Cantus high on the fingerboard,
Bassus on the lower frets;
hands changing position
above the rose?

Here there is no perfect measure
for the visitation of the plague –
no resolution
for figures on a ground –

only the memory of how
you brooded over my body;
and the speaking harmony
with which, beyond all music

I would stop your lips.

PAULINE STAINER

John Dowland on the Lute:
A Round of Variations

I

I have to think of curvatures and, hand
On notes, send these discoveries
From sea or land,
For they are my recoveries
From all the Continent,
Whence I search every sentiment.

II

My lute's circumference
I navigate as if a globe,
Its ribs the longitude,
Its neck proud prow.
My fingers on it now
Discovering the mood,
Its fantasy my robe
Of melancholy sense.

III

My tears the condensation of my brain,
That clear alembick that distils
The bitter, bitter drops of pain
The strain inside that wills
The grievance of a sad *pavane*.

IV

And yet in glass perfection
Will I compose a *galliard*
In crystalline connection
To *ayres* of which I am 'the Bard'.

V

And I can compose a *jigge*,
Hey ho and sprightly move
My fingers so they dig
And on the fretboard prove
More nimble than the feet
And certainly more sweet.

VI

Semper Dowland, semper dolens
Is what they say, and what I wrote
In 'tabliture for lute' the pens
Now copy so that, note for note,
And through my tears, the glassy lens,
They have the thing on which I dote
And my divisions and my graces prize:
The false astronomy of women's eyes.

VII

But for performance,
Be it song or dance,
I do prefer the print to sing
Perfection of the polished thing:
The music that perfection hears,
That melancholy music of the spheres.

N. S. THOMPSON

CLAUDIO MONTEVERDI (1567–1643)

Morning Words

In memoriam – that too
is brought to light by this red
sun hugely clearing tree-tops.

Nothing stays clear. Snowflakes bring,
ad infinitum, heaven
to earth. Many become one.

I, one, escape from many
dream-egos: *timor vitae*
makes them hesitate and hide.

I set hidden music free.
A loud voice from 1610
reaches out. *Exultavit.*

ROBIN FULTON MACPHERSON

GREGORIO ALLEGRI (1582–1652)

Harmonic

In space above the sung notes,
another, tongueless and numinous,
made out of sound's high fractions
gathering to lambency,
shimmering over the chord like ether.

No doubt that it's there: the monks
discover it time and again
as the engineer spools back through the takes:
a tone from a place where their breath
took flight to the stratosphere.

It rings at a fine glass frequency
and they know it together even as lovers
know, or as scientists, or as priests –
something discrete and unreachable
as light when it splits

on the wing of a plane in fathomless blue,
or the glint of the last
of a storm-cloud's rain
as the sun breaks through
into the tall air of the clerestory.

STUART HENSON

ORLANDO GIBBONS (1583–1625)

Orlando Gibbons

Thy voice, great Master, echoes through the soul,
While churches last, quires chant, and organs roll!

ALFRED, LORD TENNYSON

The Lute at Hawthornden Castle

I've waited in this corner, broken strings,
and not a hope of fingers. No one brings
a consort for me, no one's even heard
of Dowland, Gibbons, Campion or Byrd.

JOHN GREENING

DIETRICH BUXTEHUDE (1637–1707)

Buxtehude's Daughter

Father would say I thought Orlando Lasso
Was an epic on the old age of a hero –
He teased me horribly. But he also tried
To leave me safe and settled when he died,
Offering my hand in marriage to the best
Who came to take his seat – the musical test,
Then me, the princess of this fairy tale.
That's what he thought. To me, I was for sale
Like fading goods in a window, in our house
Sewing, to show I'd make a model spouse.

When Handel came, he found me elderly.
He was eighteen and I was twenty-eight –
The sad arithmetic of too soon, too late …
I wonder if he ever thinks of me
At night, in London. He liked my soup that day.
Strange to know someone famous far away.

Then young Bach came. He was so keen to learn
He overstayed, and I began to burn
Like a ripe candle in my room alone
Along the corridor. Which he must have known.
Father and he became so close. He knew
The parent's hope – but never called me Du.
Three months I was for sale and was not bought.

Though absent in the wood of musical thought
He must have seen my shape, at meals, because
Unwittingly I fired him for his cousin,
The young and merry one who sang.
                              And then
Father no longer walked, but flew to heaven.
I still kept house, now for his deputy.
They offered him the job and he took me,
That autumn. So I moved into the bed
Where I was born, and gave my maidenhead
In the same place – where I expect to die.

We have a cat and dog. Johann and I
Named them from operas he composed before
We met: Medea, the Euripidean whore,
And Alaric, the Gothic king. Johann
Christian Schieferdecker ist mein Mann,
Natürlich jünger – just four years, this time.
And do you ask if we had children? Nein.

I made the Elders give Johann more pay:
Organists wear their trouser-seats away –
All that sliding along the bench, you know.
When he plays Bach, he sweats a bit. I glow.

ALISTAIR ELLIOT

HENRY PURCELL (1659–95)

An Ode on the Death of Mr Henry Purcell

I

Mark how the lark and linnet sing:
     With rival notes
They strain their warbling throats,
   To welcome in the Spring.
   But in the close of night,
When Philomel begins her Heavenly lay,
   They cease their mutual spite,
   Drink in her music with delight,
And listening and silent, and silent and listening,
     And listening and silent obey.

II

So ceased the rival crew when Purcell came,
They sung no more, or only sung his fame.
Struck dumb they all admired the god-like man,
    The god-like man,
   Alas, too soon retired,
   As he too late began.

We beg not Hell our Orpheus to restore:
   Had he been there,
   Their sovereigns' fear
   Had sent him back before.
The power of harmony too well they know.
He long e'er this had tuned their jarring sphere,
   And left no Hell below.

III

The Heavenly choir, who heard his notes from high,
Let down the scale of music from the sky:
   They handed him along,
And all the way he taught, and all the way they sung.
Ye brethren of the lyre and tuneful voice,

13

Lament his lot – but at your own rejoice.
Now live secure and linger out your days.
The gods are pleased alone with Purcell's lays,
　　Nor know to mend their choice.

JOHN DRYDEN

Lines to W.L. (Mr William Linley) while he sang a song to Purcell's music

While my young cheek retains its healthful hues,
　And I have many friends who hold me dear,
　Linley! methinks, I would not often hear
Such melodies as thine, lest I should lose
All memory of the wrongs and sore distress,
　For which my miserable brethren weep!
　But should uncomforted misfortunes steep
My daily bread in tears and bitterness;
And if at Death's dread moment I should lie,
　With no belovèd face at my bed-side,
To fix the last glance of my closing eye,
　Methinks such strains, breathed by my angel-guide,
Would make me pass the cup of anguish by,
　Mix with the blest, nor know that I had died!

SAMUEL TAYLOR COLERIDGE

FRANÇOIS COUPERIN (1668–1733)

Couperin at the Keyboard

In a gallery of Versailles
François Couperin (called '*Le Grand*')
Is playing the clavecin –
Half-heard. Court Officials
Pace to and fro, whispering
Intrigues, affairs of state –
What city now the king shall lay siege to,
Or to which lady's virtue.

Cicadas, singing in Provençal heat –
The music gently tells
Of harvesters returning with their sheaves,
Of flowering orchards, or of shepherds' bagpipes;
And now of lovers' sighs, and lovers' plaining, –
And the soft swish of women's petticoats –
Mysterious barricades.

Evening draws on. The sun
and the Sun King retire.
Chandeliers are lit, and are extinguished:
Only the single candle
Upon his music-rest burns on.

The bass burrs like a dor, the treble
Like a mosquito whines and stings.
Shadows are dancing now – sour-faced prudes,
Dressed in black silk, with yellow fingers, ancient beauties,
Rouged and with false gold ringlets,
The powder-puffed and painted fop –
All the prisoners of the Cave of Spleen.

A chill wind lifts
The sails of the joyous ship
That is en voyage for Cythera. 'Haul Down!'
Cries the masked captain. The shroud descends
And, gleaming in the moonlight, for a moment
It seems a blood-fringed blade.

JOHN HEATH-STUBBS

ANTONIO VIVALDI (1678–1741)

'Yesterday Vivaldi visited me; and sold me some very expensive concertos'

He had only one tune.
And that
a thin finger on pulses:
of spring and the frost,
                        the quick turn of girls' eyes
a tune

to hold against darkness,
to fret
for trumpet, for lute
for flutes; violins
to silver the shabbiness
of many towns
the fool's bowl, the court coat,
a tune he would give:
without sorrow or freedom
again, again

            there is only one tune.

Sell it dearly to live.

ALISON BRACKENBURY

Dixit Dominus

Antonio Vivaldi is smiling with pleasure,
peering over the painted balustrade
(birds and cherubs in steep perspective
circling his head as they rise to Heaven)
on a painted ceiling – or so I imagine,
while listening to a performance
of his newly-discovered piece of music:
glorious sounds we hear together.

If those annotated sheets of paper –
fragile treasure – survived for centuries,
then inconceivable that their creator
does not enjoy this harmony
of voices and instruments, this blend
of ecstatic vibrations, now, from his cloud
in the sky, or seated beside me – both
of us sharing it, smiling with pleasure.

RUTH FAINLIGHT

Vivaldi's Bow

I've begun to finger the bow
and imagine those melancholy sighs
which trembled from his lips
on freezing Thursdays in the orphanage.

He had the patience of a cat,
the temper of a wild wind coming up the canal.
He hated most of us but sometimes his head
would still be beneath his red strands of hair.

Once I saw him pluck a swatch, thread it between
the usual horsehair, play a riff, the scales.
We would play as he stalked the rows,
stopped near a girl: she would tremble at her violin.

He'd begin scribbling a piece just for her,
for the next concert. I'd feel nauseous
because it wasn't me. My playing didn't excite
though I practised to exhaustion.

There was a turning over of the place
when the bow went missing.
I slipped it into the gap under the marble step
as I scrubbed it with my raw hands.

This my daily chore: my red hands were never
for coaxing true music out of maplewood
and spruce but they could clean and polish
marble fit for Vivaldi's shoes.

MARGARET SPEAK

JEAN-PHILIPPE RAMEAU (1683–1764)

On an Air of Rameau

To Arnold Dolmetsch

A melancholy desire of ancient things
Floats like a faded perfume out of the wires;
Pallid lovers, what unforgotten desires,
Whispered once, are retold in your whisperings?

Roses, roses, and lilies with hearts of gold,
These you plucked for her, these she wore in her breast;
Only Rameau's music remembers the rest,
The death of roses over a heart grown cold.

But these sighs? Can ghosts then sigh from the tomb?
Life then wept for you, sighed for you, chilled your breath?
It is the melancholy of ancient death
The harpsichord dreams of, sighing in the room.

ARTHUR SYMONS

JOHANN SEBASTIAN BACH (1685–1750)

Loch Music

I listen as recorded Bach
Restates the rhythms of a loch.
Through blends of dusk and dragonflies
A music settles on my eyes
Until I hear the living moors,
Sunk stones and shadowed conifers,
And what I hear is what I see,
A summer night's divinity.
And I am not administered
Tonight, but feel my life transferred
Beyond the realm of where I am
Into a personal extreme,
As on my wrist, my eager pulse
Counts out the blood of someone else.
Mist-moving trees proclaim a sense
Of sight without intelligence;
The intellects of water teach
A truth that's physical and rich.
I nourish nothing with the stars,
With minerals, as I disperse,
A scattering of quavered wash
As light against the wind as ash.

DOUGLAS DUNN

Pibroch: The Harp Tree

Pibroch, I make you a man
who could shake hands with Bach
and talk with him over a glass
of Rhenish wine.

You would walk in, with your sack
of images that are brightly dark and darkly bright,
and Bach, emerging from a labyrinthine fugue,
would greet you with warmth and pleasure. He'd pour
the Rhenish wine.

There'd be grave wings beating
in that room and happy silences
smiling to each other.

When you left, you'd return
to your crystal land of bogs and coloured rocks,
and Bach
would stretch his elbows sideways
like wings and fold them again and go back into
the labyrinth where he's never lost,
seeking, like you, the minotaur
that will crouch beside him
with his heavy horns,
with his beautiful, golden eyes.

NORMAN MacCAIG

Bach for the Cello

By mathematics we shall come to heaven.
This page the door of God's academy
for the geometer,

Where the pale lines involve a continent,
transcribe the countryside of formal light,
kindle with friction.

Passion will scorch deep in these sharp canals:
under the level moon, desire runs fast,
the flesh aches on its string,
without consummation,

Without loss.

ROWAN WILLIAMS

Homage to J. S. Bach

It is good just to think about Johann Sebastian
Bach grinding away like the mills of God,
Producing masterpieces, and legitimate children –
Twenty-one in all – and earning his bread

Instructing choirboys to sing their *ut re mi*,
Provincial and obscure. When Fame's trumpets told
Of Handel displaying magnificent wings of melody,
Setting the waters of Thames on fire with gold,

Old Bach's music did not seem to the point:
He groped in the Gothic vaults of polyphony,
Labouring pedantic miracles of counterpoint.
They did not know that the order of eternity

Transfiguring the order of the Age of Reason,
The timeless accents of super-celestial harmonies,
Filtered into time through that stupendous brain.
It was the dancing angels in their hierarchies,

Teaching at the heart of Reason that Passion existed,
And at the heart of Passion a Crucifixion,
Or when the great waves of his *Sanctus* lifted
The blind art of music into a blinding vision.

JOHN HEATH-STUBBS

Bach and the Sentry

Watching the dark my spirit rose in flood
  On that most dearest Prelude of my delight.
The low-lying mist lifted its hood,
  The October stars showed nobly in clear night.

When I return, and to real music-making,
  And play that Prelude, how will it happen then?
Shall I feel as I felt, a sentry hardly waking,
  With a dull sense of No Man's Land again?

IVOR GURNEY

Fugue

There was no irony in it,
After their nightfall arrival.
She always came shadowless now.

This time she brought one in his black
Swastika uniform. They ate
As usual at the oak table.

Then, in the yellow light's comfort
The older woman's accurate
Fingers unpinned a stepping fugue.

His words cut that afterglow calm:

'I did not believe that a Jew
Could play Bach like that, I thank you.'

LOTTE KRAMER

22

Bach's Journal for George Erdmann

[3pm Sunday 18 October 1705 near Wechmar, Thuringia; distance from
Arnstadt, 11 miles]

Allegro

We promised each other, George, when we quit Lüneburg
back in '02, that if ever again we took to the roads
looking for work or an education, we'd keep an archive
to share next time we met up in Ohrdruf or Celle,
the true value of walking consisting as much in process
as destination; so having today set out on a venture
with knapsack, notebook, and the second best violin
I call Gottlieb, I sit down to write these lines
and keep my part of the bargain. My destination
is Lübeck; my purpose there is to hear The Master,
that is, Magister Buxtehude, play, and by due diligence
comprehend one thing and another about his art.
What do the Chinese say? A thousand mile journey
begins with the first step, that's the hardest
but already I'm halfway to Gotha, delighted
at being let loose by the Boniface Fathers,
who either don't know how far away Lübeck is
or expect me to turn round the moment I get there
and head straight back for home. But vicissitude
rules on the road, and the thousand particulars
of unforeseen circumstance – appetite, energy,
weather, road surface, condition of footwear,
scope for adventure, conspire to halt progress,
shape the traveller's *rallentando*. We know this
even if the Fathers forget it, and so I am resolved
to put schedules aside, and working within the frame
of declared intentions, take each day as it comes.
There will be delays, prolongations – hours, days,
weeks, even, when mind, in search of itself,
turns on its axis, sets aside destinations, and looks
not into progress, but whereabouts. In the fields
sheaves of corn stand where reapers have thrown
themselves down in the shade, and from jugs
brought by blue-apronned women drink small beer
and drowse till the sun comes round; on the stave
of the stubble, woodwind are taking a rest,
and their horses, unhitched for an hour, peer

into oatfilled nosebags. From green verges
the piccolo trill of partridges flurries upwards
as they break cover, scurrying through the weeds
before they take flight. So nature is music,
and each day of the journey a manuscript sheet
where our travels are written; today the heart sings
and the feet sound the strong notes of contrabassi
beating steadily forward. For tomorrow, what comes
is sufficient, and although one ought never to praise
the day until evening, I say of it, *So far so good.*

JOHN GOHORRY

If Bach had been a Beekeeper
for Arvo Pärt

If Bach had been a beekeeper
he would have heard
all those notes
suspended above one another
in the air of his ear
as the differentiated swarm returning
to the exact hive
and place in the hive,
topping up the cells
with the honey of C major,
food for the listening generations,
key to their comfort
and solace of their distress
as they return and return
to those counterpointed levels
of hovering wings where
movement is dance
and the air itself
a scented garden

CHARLES TOMLINSON

A Touch of the Goldbergs

Andras Schiff playing The Goldberg Variations

Here's Andras letting the grass grow under Bach,
taking the shine off the carriage work,

seeing the wig blow away into cumulo-nimbus,
bowed over the naked tips of fingers

gliding along in the orbit of that tune
which flies apart, like the phases of the moon.

Here's Andras, I say, an old Rolls Royce
purring along in the best of taste

and I don't think Schubert was invented then
to skim the cream off his deep dark pain

but he's here in spirit. All music's here –
classic romantic pious pedantic –

in the grand old *meister*. Wouldn't you say?
Come, let's put Mahler out of his misery,

that great white elephant of Teutonic noise.
And Bruckner the Humble, down on his hands and knees.

Who's got the time? Majestic, true,
but going on and on forever and a day

as though, once Wagner sobbed, the height of things
was measured by time and a thousand violins.

Come! Let's grow up enough to listen in
to reason. Andras, play that thing again!

WILLIAM SCAMMELL

GEORGE FRIDERIC HANDEL (1685–1759)

G. F. Handel, Opus 6

Monumentality and *bidding*: words
neither yours nor mine, but like his music.
Stalwart and tender by turns, the fugues
and larghettos, staid, *bürgerlich*,
up to the wide gaunt leaps of invention.
Repetition of theme a reaffirming,
like figures in harmony with their right consorts,
with the world also, broadly understood;
each of itself a treatise of civil power,
every phrase instinct with deliberation
both upon power and towards civility.
At the rehearsing always I think of you
and fancy: with what concordance I
would thus steadily regret and regard her,
though to speak truth you are ever in my mind;
such is eros, such philia, their composure
these arias, predetermined, of our choice.

GEOFFREY HILL

Writing Rinaldo

'Yes, Mr Hill. An opera in two weeks.'
He is twenty. The librettists hate the haste.
He chops cantatas, scours Venetian scores.
How Handel would have worshipped cut and paste.

Yet it is there, as water trickles through
small fingers in the troughs of a great sea.
Sorrow for all he lost, or never found.
The piled-up plates. The icy bed, still empty.

No, you must live with these, the music says,
although the groves of wandering flutes give joy
to girls, the passing 'prentice and the Prince.
Work! Leave your money to the coachman's boy.

'Yes, Mr Hill. I scored for fireworks.'
Lit faces cheer, although his critics rage
at painted waves. They mourn – as I do, too –
that promised horses never reached the stage.

Magician! Living sparrows twitter trees
beside castrati. No, I do not know.
His trumpets flare. The Saracens take flight.
The Siren rises from the undertow.

Already a young whale in music's sea,
he will return, with his own company,

huge dinners. His accounts are never wrong.
Breathless, he hums the slim girl's misery.
Lashed to himself, he scrawls the Siren's song.

ALISON BRACKENBURY

Epigram on the Feuds between Handel and Bononcini

Some say, compar'd to Bononcini
That Mynheer Handel's but a ninny;
Others aver, that he to Handel
Is scarcely fit to hold a candle.
Strange all this difference should be
'Twixt Tweedle-dum and Tweedle-dee!

JOHN BYROM

DOMENICO SCARLATTI (1685–1757)

From *Briggflatts*

It is time to consider how Domenico Scarlatti
condensed so much music into so few bars
with never a crabbed turn or congested cadence,
never a boast or a see-here; and stars and lakes
echo him and the copse drums out his measure,
snow peaks are lifted up in moonlight and twilight
and the sun rises on an acknowledged land.

BASIL BUNTING

CHRISTOPH WILLIBALD von GLUCK
(1714–87)

Scottish Play

*… a penny Poet whose first making was the miserable stolne story of Macdeol,
or Macdobeth, or Mac-somewhat, for I am sure a Mac it was, though I never
had the maw to see it …*

William Kemp, *Kemp's Nine Days' Wonder*, 1600

Others would rather stammer, and beg your pardon,
Than name that thunderbolt of *opera seria*
Conducted by the 'gentle sorcerer', Gluck,
Which struck the national alto, Kathleen Ferrier,
Although she tweaked the curtain, thrice, for luck
In 1953, at Covent Garden.

A 'wooden actress' – that would be our Kath,
Strumming the plyboard lyre; but when she sang,
So mixed of man and woman, love and death,
Sacred, *heimlich*, and operatic breath,
The house in high forgetfulness forgot
Whom it should mourn or pity, and for what.

And though the wings spared her the customary
Backslap and 'Break a leg!' for her own good,
Her *ca-cancerous* right hip snapped where she stood –
As she recalled in hospital, pillowed and propped
In eiderdown, *I wanted a soft manhole
To open up immediately and devour me* –

Still, still, she made them carry her back on stage
To sing his tortured air or aria,
The plum 'Che farò senza Euridice',
Which Gluck implored the original Orfeo,
A bull castrato, to perform 'as if
You're having two-thirds of your leg sawn off'.

MICK IMLAH

FRANZ JOSEPH HAYDN (1732–1809)

Small Fanfare for H. C. Robbins Landon
'Io la Musica Son'

For a moment there I thought
I was pounding my chest,
I thought I was sounding brass.

Time rounded out, time after time,
in Haydn's number ninety-nine.
Earth, sun, stars, moon
deep in the belly of the tune.

For a moment there I thought
the planets stayed in their courses.

WILLIAM SCAMMELL

To Haydn

Who is the mighty master that can trace
Th'eternal lineaments of Nature's face?
Mid endless dissonance, what mortal ear
Could e'er her peal of perfect concord hear?
Answer, oh, Haydn! strike the magic chord!
And, as thou strik'st, reply and proof afford.
　Whene'er thy genius, flashing native fire,
Bids the soul tremble with the trembling lyre,
The hunter's clatt'ring hoof, the peasant-shout,
The warrior-onset, or the battle's rout,
Din, clamour, uproar, murder's midnight knell,
Hyena shrieks, the war-whoop, scream and yell –
All sounds, however mingled, strange, uncouth,
Resolve to fitness, system, sense and truth!
To others, noise and jangling; but to thee
'Tis one grand solemn swell of endless harmony.
　When dark and unknown terrors intervene,
And men aghast survey the horrid scene;
Then, when rejoicing fiends flit, gleam and scowl,
And bid the huge tormented tempest howl;
When fire-fraught thunders roll, and whirlwinds rise,

And earthquakes bellow to the frantic skies,
Till the distracted ear, in racking gloom,
Suspects the wreck of worlds, and gen'ral doom:
Then Haydn stands, collecting Nature's tears,
And consonance sublime amid confusion hears.

THOMAS HOLCROFT

A fiat *for Joseph Haydn*

When the Count says *I have four friends, amateur*
players; write something for them to perform
next time they come over to Weinzierl,
suppose these the thoughts of Herr Haydn,
eighteen years old, shabbily-dressed, hungry.

Imagine a man as a man's life,
and the events of a man's life as notes
on a stave that is also the fingerboard
of the magical instrument of his life,
tuned, toned, Stradivarius resonant;

then add to that voice another with which
it engages in parody, echo,
partition, the thrust and parry of discourse
only through which imagining mind comes
to apprehend implication. Then bring

beneath both the deep, dark tsunami swell
of the cello heart, languorous sometimes,
sonorous, always autumnal, singing
with a rising or falling cadence
solemn reminders of death in the bass clef.

Last of all, darker than fiddles, brighter
than cello, let viola mediate,
chart the overlooked, taken-for-granted,
hard-to-find side-streets of common ground,
where talk is an easy vernacular.

He busies himself with manuscripts, stays
up all hours in the barn, working. He calls
them his *String Quartets*, the first of their kind.
Where accidents are convergent, he thinks,
there will always be scope for invention.

JOHN GOHORRY

After the Celibacy of Summer

After the celibacy of summer,
the last movement of Haydn's 'Farewell'
has freed each instrument in turn,
and now they are making off

across the lawns of the Esterházy palace,
one at a swallow-tailed time:
the wanton oboes and the horns,
engorged bassoons, priapic strings,
the carnal bass drum *con abbandono*.

They leave in their wake
the dry old kapellmeister,
strewn strawberries, crushed canapés,
a clatter of upturned chairs,
a smatter of surprised applause
as the fat-arsed cello
crashes an ornamental pond.

Meanwhile the wives of Eisenstadt
pay scant attention to their prayers.
One turns a mattress, another a curl.
With heightened colour and tapping feet
they shuck their silks and soak themselves.
Tonight it will be chamber music.

TONY ROBERTS

ANTONIO SALIERI (1750–1825)

Mozart and Salieri

Salieri encountered Mozart;
   Took him friendly by the arm,
And smiled a thin-lipped ambiguous smile.
   This was Italian charm.

Mozart observed the smile of Salieri
   But was not enough observant,
(For the Angel of Death had called already
   In the guise of an upper servant).

'Maestro,' said Salieri. 'Dear Maestro,
   It is happy that we met.'
('We'll end this sharp boy's tricks,' he thought
   'He'll not get by – not yet!')

'And as for that post of kapellmeister
   We'll do what we can do.'
But something black within him whispered:
   'He is greater, is greater than you.

'He is great enough to oust you, one day,
   And take your place at Court.'
('Not if Salieri is Salieri,'
   Salieri thought.)

'It is happy that we met,' said Salieri
   'I wish I could ask you to dine –
But I have, alas, a pressing engagement.
   You will stay for a glass of wine?'

No one carried Mozart to nobody's grave
   And the skies were glazed and dim
With a spatter of out-of-season rain
   (Or the tears of the Seraphim).

Then two stern angels stood by that grave
   Saying: 'Infidel, Freemason,
We are taking your soul where it willed to be judged
   At the throne of Ultimate Reason.'

But the Queen of the Night in coloratura
  Horrors trilled at the sun,
For she looked at the soul of Wolfgang Amadeus
  And she knew she had not won.

They lifted that soul where the great musicians
  In contrapuntal fires
Through unlimited heavens of order and energy
  Augment the supernal choirs.

And the spirit of Johann Sebastian, harrowed
  With abstract darts of love,
Escorted the terrible child Mozart
  Through courteous mansions above.

And hundred-fisted Handel erected
  Great baroque arches of song
As the Cherubim and the Seraphim
  Bandied Mozart along.

But Mozart looked back again in compassion
  Below the vault of the stars
To where the body of Beethoven battered
  Its soul on the prison bars.

Successful Salieri lay dying –
  But now his reason was gone –
In a chamber well-fitted with Louis Seize furniture,
  But dying, dying alone.

Then two small devils, like surpliced choirboys,
  Like salamanders in black and red,
Extracted themselves from the fluttering firelight
  And stood beside the bed.

And they sang to him then in two-part harmony,
  With their little, eunuchoid voices:
'You have a pressing engagement, Salieri,
  In the place of no more choices.'

So they hauled down his soul and put it away
  In a little cushioned cell
With stereophonic gramophones built into the walls –
  And he knew that this must be Hell.

Salieri sat there under the chandeliers
  (But never the sun or the moon)
With nothing to listen to from eternity to eternity
  But his own little tinkling tune.

JOHN HEATH-STUBBS

WOLFGANG AMADEUS MOZART
(1756–91)

K595 (Mozart)

Sometimes there breaks in on us a new dance,
darkness touched alight, something going straight
to the bone of our being. For instance,
circumventing thought, total and complete,
Piano Concerto Twenty Seven
unselves our worldliness, undoes our sleep,
a song brought back from the edge of Heaven,
a simple shape of notes that makes us weep.

SEÁN STREET

Kosovo Surprised by Mozart

(Bernard Roberts playing K533, 11 April 1999)

Lovely chromatic Mozart, talk to me
in your language of intimate, arithmetical
progression. Perform with this performer.
Hold that diminished seventh's cutting edge
close against the dominant until it
skylarks away from the tonic's expectant
cages to a charmed high of almost
imperceptible *rallentando*, only to
circle back lightly into the right key.

Why does what is known of happiness,
like sadness, find insignia in harmony?
Your genes were a template of musical
grammar from the hour of your birth.
You must have translated straight from
sensation into sound, ignoring the tongue's
barbed wire at disputed borders. How young
you were, how unfinished your work of
spinning tempi into timelessness.

Easy it may be to bless and be blessed
in the *terra cognita* of Pythagoras, but
who lives there long? Young hungry hours can't
help but devour us, hacking from east to west
through this eleventh day, fourth month, last year
of the twentieth century. An uninhabited body is
slashed and displayed on a pole. It's not unusual
for flesh to be pummelled, pistol-whipped,
groin-kicked, machine-gunned under arrest.

For news is the news, and our cameras favour
burying sufferers alive in rewindable footage.
And your spirit? Escaped long ago in a passion
of inky dots. It's for ten live fingers to decode you –
leapfrogging over the rubble, the incurable hospital,
the wreck of the temple, the cries and imploring hands.
We accuse you, Herr Mozart, of not representing our age.
Simplified, rarefied, perfectionist as ever,
punish us in the key of F major.

ANNE STEVENSON

Mozart's Horn Concertos

Not for war or hunting cry
Is this; it gentles down the heart,
So there's no question asking 'Why

Does man exist?' God gave him art,
And God is proved in every note
And every sound takes its own part

In what a young composer wrote
Who ended in a pauper's grave.
The disc is on, the patterns float

And I feel back at some strange start
And marvel at what Mozart gave.

ELIZABETH JENNINGS

Exsultate, Jubilate

The talented young soprano singing Mozart
in our church is pregnant. Her white silk
is stretched so tight it shows an edge of corset
and a smooth curve not dimpled by a kick –
although she piercingly sings 'Exsultate'.
He should be skipping 'like the little hills'
inside – even if I am weeping as she sings
into the wind of history, 'Jubilate'.

The small bald competent man with the trumpet smiles
looking at her. Somehow the leaping strings
bring me the Roman mother who called in
a legionary band to make her son
(unborn) a hero. What will this child do
so near her voice now giving the command
to jump for joy? Live life fortissimo?
Or prefer silence to all public sound?

ALISTAIR ELLIOT

Cadenza

I've played it so often it's hardly me who plays.
We heard it that morning in Alexandria,
Or tried to, on that awful radio.
I was standing at the balustrade,
Watching the fish stalls opening on the quay,
The horizon already rippling in the heat.
She'd caught a snatch of Mozart, and was fishing
Through the static for the BBC
But getting bouzoukis, intimate Arabic,
All drowned beneath that soft roar, like the ocean's.
'Give it up,' I said, 'The tuner's broken.'
And then she crossed the room and kissed me. Later,
Lying in the curtained light, she whispered
She'd something to tell me. When all at once,
The tidal hiss we'd long since ceased to notice
Stopped. A flautist inhaled. And there it was,
The end of K285a,
Dubbed like a budget soundtrack on our big scene.
Next day I got the music out and learned it.

I heard it again in London a few months later,
The night she called me from the hospital.
'I've lost it,' she said, 'It happens ...' and as she spoke
Those days in Egypt and other days returned,
Unsummoned, a tide of musics, cities, voices,
In which I drifted, helpless, disconsolate.
What did I mourn? It had no name, no sex,
'It might not even have been yours,' she said,
Or do I just imagine that she said that?

The next thing I recall, I'm in the dark
Outside St Michael's Church on Highgate Hill,
Coloured lights are strung across the portico,
Christmas lights. It's snowing on me,
And this very same cadenza – or near enough –
Rasps through a tubercular PA.
How did I get here?

Consider that radio, drifting through frequencies,
Suddenly articulate with Mozart.
Consider the soloist playing that cadenza,
Borne to the coda by his own hands.

MICHAEL DONAGHY

Mozart Playing Billiards

Wolfie drifting round the table
so casual; he had a rhythm,
you know, that cue was part of his arm.
I don't suppose he was even in here
that often, but he was the kind they all
watch: such a sweet mover.

He could have been great: I told him so,
only his heart was never in it.
Playing just relaxed him; helped him write.
You'd see him cock an ear to the click
of the balls; then he'd grab a cue
and tap out tunes, for God's sake.

Catchy tunes, too; folk hummed them
all round town: he had class, Wolfie,
whatever he did … Well, I tell a lie,
there was one thing. That man,
I swear, had the foulest mouth on him.
I'd have to insist, every so often,

please Wolfie, less of the effing.
Odd, isn't it? Give him a harpsichord
or a cue, he was magic; yet every word
was an embarrassment. Well, there you are,
a man can't be good at everything.
… God, though, he could have been a player.

SHEENAGH PUGH

The Unsung Mechanisms

I am sick sick sick sick sick of being fobbed off
with snuffboxes, enamel trinkets and watches
one after another instead of my proper fee.

What need have I for a clock in every pocket
repeating on me, *me* – the finest timekeeper of all –
all Mannheim at least? Punctuality. It does nothing

but demean. Oh there are nights when the whole sky
revolves like a timepiece in my hand, when constellations
suspend themselves in a matrix of silence,

patient as icicles waiting to melt into sound.
You know how sometimes a fugue presents itself
and all its possibilities in an instant …?

I wear myself out, working out the workings of each
inevitability: the balance wheel, the hairspring coiled
like a butterfly's tongue, the jewelled intricacies.

Tonight it's freezing – all glockenspiel and glass
harmonica, inaudible to everyone but me,
and I must single-handedly transcribe the stars,

must find each one its place in these ruled staves,
must bring down the chiming of the spheres
and shackle the celestial in inky rings –

minim and semibreve. Must put heaven behind bars.
Being human – utterly, unutterably human – I risk
everything, and know my work will come to be seen

as one provisional resolution. Only the stars
are constant. My tears congeal. Ah Constanze
think of my scores as atlases of time, of me as Atlas.

GREGORY WARREN WILSON

K563

As on most fine summer Sundays
we are breakfasting outdoors with our books.
This morning it is one of the Divertimenti
keeps the neighbours to themselves.
Now I can remember that man's name – Puchberg –
who funded Mozart when his wife was ill
        and the money coming in
wasn't covering the bills.
This is Vienna in 1788 in sunlight.

What are we supposed to do?
I open a conversation about Mozart
and you look up from the Penguin biography.
        The sky is a Prussian blue
and our back-yard garden is lit with music.

We are not yet thirty, and our lives
        are just about to start.
There is someone new, but that
is not why you are leaving. The cat,
who will be staying, stalks a daytime moth;
two stray poppies add a splash of colour.

It is very civilised. We are parting like friends.
On the breeze the churchbell tolls eleven.
Coming so far he won't arrive till three,
but your cases are already packed in case.
I've not slept properly for days
and now I need to be awake I find I'm dozing.
      When the record finishes
it is the hairfine crack in a teacup, ticking,
or a clock, perhaps, loud and very exact.

PETER SANSOM

Lines to a Movement in Mozart's E-Flat Symphony

          Show me again the time
          When in the Junetide's prime
      We flew by meads and mountains northerly! –
Yea, to such freshness, fairness, fulness, fineness, freeness,
          Love lures life on.

          Show me again the day
          When from the sandy bay
      We looked together upon the pestered sea! –
Yea, to such surging, swaying, sighing, swelling, shrinking,
          Love lures life on.

          Show me again the hour
          When by the pinnacled tower
      We eyed each other and feared futurity! –
Yea, to such bodings, broodings, beatings, blanchings, blessings,
          Love lures life on.

          Show me again just this:
          The moment of that kiss
      Away from the prancing folk, by the strawberry-tree! –
Yea, to such rashness, ratheness, rareness, ripeness, richness,
          Love lures life on.

THOMAS HARDY

LUDWIG VAN BEETHOVEN (1770–1827)

Barclays Bank and Lake Baikal

The bank walks in at half past seven, dressed and unembarrassed
by its sponsorship of Beethoven, the best

of music, *Hammerklavier*, here in its own town
Darlington.

Demidenko, Nikolai, in concert, self-exiled,
walks out of another world

like one who's wandered, handkerchief in hand, into the town
to watch the hammer of the auctioneer come down

and then, instead, plays Beethoven
as if he were alone.

He looks like Silas Marner so intent upon his two thick leather
        bags of gold
he lost the world

we live in: cough, cold, cufflink and the ache and pain
of bone.

It looks as if the light, Siberian, is breaking slowly over Lake Baikal,
as if our ship of fools

and bankers, borne upon the waters
of a bare

adagio, may founder in a quite uncalled for and unsponsored
sea of solitude.

But not tonight, dour Demidenko, dealer in another world's
dear gold –

for Darlington's recalled. At ten to ten
the bank picks up its leather bag, walks out again.

GILLIAN ALLNUTT

Sonata

Evening. The wind rising.
The gathering excitement
of the leaves, and Beethoven
on the piano, chords reverberating
in our twin being.
                          'What is life?'
pitifully her eyes
asked. And I who was no seer
took hold of her loth hand
and examined it and was lost
like a pure mathematician
in its solution: strokes
cancelling strokes; angles
bisected; the line of life deviating
from the line of the head; a way
that was laid down for her to walk
which was not my way.
                          While the music
went on and on with chromatic
insistence, passionately proclaiming
by the keys' moonlight in the darkening
drawing-room how our art is our meaning.

R. S. THOMAS

From *Epilogue to Lessing's Laocoön*

Miserere, Domine!
The words are utter'd, and they flee.
Deep is their penitential moan,
Mighty their pathos, but 'tis gone.
They have declared the spirit's sore
Sore load, and words can do no more.
Beethoven takes them – those two
Poor, bounded words – and makes them new;
Infinite makes them, makes them young;
Transplants them to another tongue,
Where they can now, without constraint,
Pour all the soul of their complaint,
And roll adown a channel large

43

The wealth divine they have in charge.
Page after page of music turn,
And still they live and still they burn,
Eternal, passion-fraught, and free –
Miserere, Domine!

MATTHEW ARNOLD

Arioso Dolente

(for my grandchildren when they become grandparents)

Mother, who read and thought and poured herself into me;
she was the jug and I was the two-eared cup.
How she would scorn today's 'show-biz inanity,
democracy twisted, its high ideals sold up!'
   Cancer filched her voice, then cut her throat.
      Why is it
    none of the faces in this family snapshot
      looks upset?

Father, who ran downstairs as I practised the piano;
barefooted, buttoning his shirt, he shouted 'G,
D-natural, C-*flat*! *Dolente, arioso.*
Put all the griefs of the world in that change of key.'
   Who then could lay a finger on his sleeve
      to distress him with
 'One day, Steve, two of your well-taught daughters
      will be deaf.'

Mother must be sitting, left, on the porch-set,
you can just see her. My sister's on her lap.
And that's Steve confiding to his cigarette
something my mother's mother has to laugh at.
    The screened door twangs, slamming
      on its sprung hinge.
   Paint blisters on the steps; iced tea, grasscuttings,
     elm flowers, mock orange …

A grand June evening, like this one, not too buggy,
unselfquestioning midwestern, maybe 1951.
And, of course, there in my grandmother's memory
lives just such another summer – 1890 or 91.
    Though it's not on her mind now/then.

44

No, she's thinking of
the yeast-ring rising in the oven. Or how *any* shoes
irritate her bunion.

Paper gestures, pictures, newsprint laughter.
And after the camera winks and makes its catch,
the decibels drain away *for ever and ever*.
No need to say 'Look!' to these smilers on the porch,
'Grandmother will have her stroke,
and you, mother, will nurse her.'
Or to myself, this woman died paralysed-dumb, and that one
dumb from cancer.

Sufficient unto the day ... Grandmother, poor and liturgical,
whose days were duties, stitches in the tea-brown blanket
she for years crocheted, its zigzag of yellow wool,
her grateful offering, her proof of goodness to present,
gift-wrapped, to Our Father in Heaven. 'Accept,
O Lord, this best-I-can-make-it soul.'
And He: 'Thou good and faithful servant, lose thyself
and be whole.'

Consciousness walks on tiptoe through what happens.
So much is felt, so little of it said.
But ours is the breath on which the past depends.
'What happened' is what the living teach the dead,
who, smilingly, lost to their lost concerns,
in grey on grey,
are all of them deaf, blind, unburdened
by today.

As if our recording selves, our mortal identities,
could be cupped in a concave universe or lens,
ageless at all ages, cleansed of memories,
not minding that meaningful genealogy extends
no further than mind's flash images reach back.
As for what happens next,
let all the griefs of the world
find keys for that.

ANNE STEVENSON

Opus 131

Opus 131 in C Sharp Minor
Opened the great door
In the air, and through it
Flooded horror. The door in the hotel room
And the curtain at the window and even
The plain homely daylight blocking the window
Were in the wrong dimension
To shut it out. The counterpoint pinned back
The flaps of the body. Naked, faceless,
The heart panted there, like a foetus.
Where was the lifeline music? What had happened
To consolation, prayer, transcendence –
To the selective disconnecting
Of the pain centre? Dark insects
Fought with their instruments
Scampering through your open body
As if you had already left it. Beethoven
Had broken down. You strained listening
Maybe for divorce to be resolved
In the arithmetic of vibration
To pure zero, for the wave-particles
To pronounce on the unimportance
Of the menopause. Beethoven
Was trying to repair
The huge constellations of his silence
That flickered and glinted in the wind.
But the notes, with their sharp faces,
Were already carrying you off,
Each with a different bit, into the corners
Of the Universe.

TED HUGHES

Für Elise

On her answering machine, Beethoven's *petite phrase*
I heard a hundred times a day when I was eight or nine
and my sister, five years older, practising for her exam.
She took her grades so seriously each night brought a migraine;
sometimes she'd stop and shake with fury after just three bars
if she wasn't perfect. And now I wish that I'd learnt too
(I refused the lessons, the *piano was hers*, like the phone)
since even listening can show me for the fraud I am,
a 'music-lover' who can't read a note, and barely understands
the structure of the simplest piece, like this one – let alone
the later string quartets; or, how unhappiness and pain
are made safe and beautiful, far from what I knew
then, and can't handle now – unsmiling silence, my mother's sign
of disappointment; the aching head in shaking hands.

ALAN JENKINS

The Composer's Ear-Trumpet

Pick me up. Put me to your ear.
No. The other way. Are you deaf?
Now, you should be able to hear
baton-taps and then the uncoiling clef

of the old tunes,
fury, fugue, double-basses like sea-swell,
molten brass, staid bassoons,
the old music caught in a shell.

A voice cries from a dead planet.
Shouting through clouds of hair-powder,
it's obdurate, deaf as granite:
'Louder. Louder. Louder.'

OLIVER REYNOLDS

Concerto

Miss pianist bows her lovely back
under the hail of notes
that she's returning, slightly damaged,
to Beethoven.

The audience puts on looks
of exquisite thoughtfulness. How lucky
to have horn-rimmed glasses
in the middle of your skull.

On the podium, the conductor
is a cobra half reared
from a basket. How stupid
not to know who's the charmer.

Beethoven knows nothing of such things
ever since he became
deafer
than deafness.

NORMAN MacCAIG

NICCOLÒ PAGANINI (1782–1840)

Paganini and the Powers of Darkness

She swore an angels' chorus
swarmed her pallet bearing
sycamore slats for the belly
of her unborn son's violin.
When others claimed to hear
Satan's heartbeat in his sweet
tremolo, she remembered ebony
for Niccolò's fingerboard landing
like grace around her. It gleamed
with the Lord's truant light.

He said she was not to speak
of that, nor of his packer
father playing mandolin
to the rapt child curled
by the fire. She must lock
his early scores in a strongbox
under her bed. Let them believe
a demon composed the music
in blood. Let them weep
for the brilliance of his
fiendish cadenzas that flickered
like the tongue of flame.

An odor of sulphur rose
from the wings, sharp
as the whip of his bow.
Despite a hint of vapor
from below, no one stirred.
In a vault under the dark
stage he tuned his strings
to the devil's chosen pitch.
By shadow of candlelight, voice
hoarsened with cancer, he practiced
his sinister pizzicatos.

FLOYD SKLOOT

JOHN FIELD (1782–1837)

John Field

Born beneath cathedral bells,
he heard their morning and evening *Pathetique*.
The cheerfulness of their clanging metals
came gusting to his doorstep.

The boy from Golden Lane
with an ear for melancholy.
The idol of Paris, Vienna, St Petersburg.
The pensive maker of the transcendent nocturne.

Moscow congratulated him
for his lullabies to soothe the nineteenth century.
Night after night the privileged and prosperous
came to hear and applaud

John Field who made piano-chords
sound like the rise and fall of breath,
who when he played seemed to bend
and whisper to his easeful melody.

GERARD SMYTH

Field

Think of those artists who will never
escape the shadow of one they had
the bad luck to precede, who did

it first but not quite as stunningly
as the name we now remember. John
Field, for example, 'inventor of

the Nocturne', who nodded off while
Chopin opened the five-bar gate
and walked all over him.

JOHN GREENING

FRANZ SCHUBERT (1797–1828)

Beautiful Place

from *Triptych for Music*

Only one beautiful place, says music as it thrums
chords to itself. When I think of the beautiful place
I imagine it with Schubert. No one comes
and no one goes in the great organic palace,

everyone is alone. My parents are asleep
somewhere in the cellars, and the wind slips
through rooms several storeys deep.
I'm in the earth with them. Something grips

my heart. A violin is scribbling light
over the dark floor. These images are
pointless, I know. Music has no need

of what we say or think about it. Tonight
my mother is dead for the twenty-fifth year.
Schubert tiptoes through the house as I read.

GEORGE SZIRTES

The Piano

The last bus sighs through the stops of the sleeping suburb
and he's home again with a click of keys, a step on the stairs.
I see him again, shut in the upstairs sitting-room
in that huge Oxfam overcoat, one hand shuffling
through the music, the other lifting the black wing.

My light's out in the room he was born in. In the hall
the clock clears its throat and counts twelve hours
into space. His scales rise, falter and fall back –
not easy to fly on one wing, even for him
with those two extra digits he was born with.

I should have known there'd be music as he flew, singing,
and the midwife cried out, 'Magic fingers!' A small variation,
born with more, like obsession. They soon fell,
tied like the cord, leaving a small scar fading
on each hand like a memory of flight.

Midnight arpeggios, Bartók, Schubert. I remember,
kept in after school, the lonely sound of a piano lesson
through an open window between-times, sun on the lawn
and everyone gone, the piece played over and over
to the metronome of tennis. Sometimes in the small hours,

after two, the hour of his birth, I lose myself listening
to that little piece by Schubert, perfected in the darkness
of space where the stars are so bright they cast shadows,
and I wait for that waterfall of notes, as if
two hands were not enough.

GILLIAN CLARKE

Music for Invasive Surgery

Hush is unnecessary.
Surgeons operate on the ear
to the sound of string quartets.

Hands make division on a ground:
moving parts are revealed
like a skeleton clock.

Why is excision
the most haunting
of disciplines –

the divining of affliction
never appropriate –
the music to which the unicorn kneels

death and the maiden?

PAULINE STAINER

Claire, Playing Schubert

'ye lovely ladyes with youre longe fingres'

This is the kind of poem I never write,
dropping musicians' names. But where else
is there to turn, but back down the path
that leads to childhood and those dreamt despairs.
After the power of the closing bars
that made you thrust down at the keys, then lean
back to make the passion keep its distance,
your hands stay fixed, reluctant at the end
to leave their scene of triumph.
                              Dream-children,
of course. I've never heard you play. I know you less
than I know Uchida whom I saw once
taking the stairs two steps at a time,
hurrying to play Schubert in the Festival Hall,
on the floor above where I was reading.

BERNARD O'DONOGHUE

Winterreise

He makes a winter journey
(Goodnight, goodnight, my love);
And howling dogs shall see him pass,
A crow keep watch above.

The will-o'-the-wisp shall light him,
His shadow lag behind;
Inconstancy like a weathercock
Shall beat about his mind.

He'd melt the snow with weeping
To where she trod the grass –
But weary dawns shall mock his dream
With frost-flowers on the glass;

And through the boneyard whistling
(No grave to hide his grief)
The wind shall dash his hope away,
A final, quivering leaf.

The linden-tree shall whisper,
The fingerpost shall tell:
Put out the light, like your delusive
Suns, and say farewell –

Or with the organ-grinder
Go patient, barefoot, numb,
Sing to a single, faltering tune,
And take things as they come.

HUMPHREY CLUCAS

For M. S.
Singing Frühlingsglaube in 1945
Nun muss sich alles, alles wenden

Here are the Schubert Lieder. Now begin.

First the accompaniment,
Heart-known and heaven-sent
And so divinely right
The inmost spirit laughs with sure delight.

And now the fountain of the melody.

To your forgiven fields I am entered in,
Spring of my adolescence, Spring of the world,
Where every secret lime-leaf is unfurled,
Where all's made well again, yet more's to be –

Then why this misery?

Because, O enemy alien heart, we fear
That you are lost on your demoniac shore,
And we deny that in your music – here
Is your unchanged, unchanging innocent core.

FRANCES CORNFORD

From *The Unfinished*

Those last few days
of drug-drowse, coma-comfort,
friends came, if not as many
as before, to keep her company,
to talk, to weep.
At each arriving voice,
I thought I saw
a faint, fleeting
muscular effort
adjust her mouth and jaw
as if in greeting,
as if for a kiss.

But how could that have been?

I talked, too, read aloud
from her favourite Yeats,
or played the last, great
Schubert quartets –
the one in G
that, with whole-hearted
ambivalence,
weighs in the balance
the relative merits
of major and minor
and struggles to postpone the choice.

While I cultivated
my clumsy, husbandly
bedside manner,
she lay as her nurses had arranged her:
reposeful beloved,
stark stranger –
or something in between.

CHRISTOPHER REID

HECTOR BERLIOZ (1803–69)

Rehearsing for the Final Reckoning in Boston

During the Berlioz *Requiem* in Symphony Hall
which takes even longer than extra innings
in big league baseball, this restless Jewish agnostic
waits to be pounced on, jarred by the massed fanfare
of trombones and trumpets assembling now in the second
balcony, left side, right side, and at the rear.

Behind them, pagan gods in their niches
acoustically oversee this most Christian
of orchestrations: the resting Satyr
of Praxiteles, faun with infant Bacchus,
Apollo Belvedere, Athena, Diana
of Versailles with early greyhound.

When the wild mélange cries out
Dies irae, all of our bared hearts pulse
under Ozawa's baton. He is lithe as a cat,
nimble as Nureyev, another expatriate.
But even Ozawa dressed in white sweats
cannot save us up here in peanut heaven, or save

patrons downstairs in the best seats canted back
for the view, who wear the rapt faces of the fifties
tilted to absorb the movie on the 3-D screen.
Naught shall remain unavenged, sings the chorus.
What trembling there shall be when we rise again
to answer at the throne. That's all of us

since Adam, standing on one another's shoulders
three or four deep, I should imagine,
acrobats of the final reckoning.
And what terror awaits those among us
whose moral priorities are unattached
to Yahweh, Allah, Buddha, Christ:

forgiving without praying for forgiveness,
the doing unto others, scrubbing toilets,
curbing lust, not taking luck for granted?
Are the doubters reckoned up or just passed over?
Hector was almost passed over, his *Requiem*
unplayed, save for a general killed in battle ...

How should one dress for the Day of Judgment?
At a working rehearsal the chorus is motley,
a newborn *fin de siècle* in t-shirts and jeans.
But what will they wear when the statues have crumbled
in 2094? Brasses and massive tympani close
the *Lacrymosa*. Metallic spittle is hot in my throat.

Now we enter the key of G major, the Lamb
of God key of catharsis and resolution.
Like a Janus head looking backward and forward,
pockmarked by doubt I slip between cymbals
to the other side of the century where our children's
children's children ride out on the ranting brasses.

MAXINE KUMIN

FELIX MENDELSSOHN (1809–47)

Mendelssohn at Thirty-Eight

I look back on the promise of my youth
(*Felix the Fortunate*) and am so tired.
A boy in auburn ringlets playing fugues
for old Goethe, a boy with liquid fire
in his hands! I glimpsed myself in glacier
wind and flood waters under the slender
Devil's Bridge. I loved the wild allegro,
the clack of trains, wind in a seaside cave.
Swiss sunlight, Monti Albani's sweet air,
Loch Lomond. I found music everywhere.
Now some mornings I am too weak to fold
back my bedsheets. There is nothing I crave
as much as silence. Not even pine trees,
the rich smell of old stones with moss upon
them, or the sight of snowy peaks would please
me. Quiet, like the moment before song
stretched out forever. Stillness, that instant
before strings quiver. This is what I want.

FLOYD SKLOOT

FRYDERYK CHOPIN (1810–49)

Chopin in London

Poor Fritz, poor Fritzchen, Frédéric Chopin, I
Man my resources to play all the night through,
Flex my wrist as a singer might draw in breath
Pausing before her first irresolute note –
For whom shall I sing but you, old cimbalom,
Simpleton of my wanderings, confidante
Like me played out by circumstance? – slender frame
More or less sound, a few strings snapped inside
Waiting for some Pleyel to refashion them.

Play to yourself, for yourself, while the gay throng
Murmur together, impatient for the end –
It will come, it will come – yellow, shrivelled, cold,
Three layers of flannel under my clothes, still
No bigger than a boy, shrunk over the keys,
Nothing left but my longer-than-ever nose
And a third finger desperately out of play.

Dowagers, dowried debutantes, dowdy belles,
They've got their grip on me – I can't shake them off –
Introduce me all over – who knows to whom? –
Chatter while I perform and then play themselves
Soulful and inaccurate, watching their hands –
Lank dried-up green-and-yellow countesses,
Scottish ladies who whistle to the guitar,
Mrs Grote, grotesque, with her baritone voice
Asking me up three flights of steps to her box,
We chatted like the goose and the sucking pig
For I could speak no English and she no French –
The continuous round of dinners, concerts, balls,
Surrounded by people, feeling so alone,
More bored than ever, bored, incredibly bored.

If London were not so black, its people dull,
Or if it could lose its smell of soot and fog,
I might even now dare to open my mouth
In this, your so-dear city. But I get up
Coughing myself to death, take soup in my room,
Get Daniel to dress me, gasp all day, not fit
For anything until dinner. Then to stop

At table with these cattle, watching them talk,
Listening to them drink – oh, good kind souls,
So ugly and so alarming, let me breathe,
Understand what is said to me, live to greet
One or two friendly faces – those that are left.

PHILIP HOBSBAUM

In Chopin's Garden

I remember the scarlet setts
Of the little-frequented highway
From Warsaw to the West
And Chopin's house, one Sunday.

I remember outside the windows,
As the pianist plucked a ring
From her thin white finger, the rows
Of unanchored faces waiting,

And a climbing vapour, storm-wrack
Wreathing up, heavy with fruit,
Darkened the skies at their back
On the old invasion-route.

Masovia bows its birches
Resignedly. Again
A rapid army marches
Eastward over the plain,

And fast now it approaches.
Turbulence, agonies,
As the poised musician broaches
The polonaise, storm from the keys.

See them, ennobled by
The mass and passage, these
Faces stained with the sky,
Supple and fluid as trees.

DONALD DAVIE

ROBERT SCHUMANN (1810–56)

Dichterliebe

The young man sings with such rich exactness
From the whitewashed chancel in the sun:
The German poet is breaking his heart with idealism.
The singer's woman looks on, slim and beautiful.

Ich liebe dich! It is real between them:
They hold hands with such excitement afterwards.

Wonderful thrilling songs! Gone with the last humming wire.
Heine's grief buried in a monstrous coffin, he said.

At home again, I read you the words of the songs in the sun,
Then cut them up with scissors to amuse the baby.
As we walk in the long grass you place my hand on your breast:
The garden is transformed into a green arena of expectancy.
I recall the music strumming on, the declamation,
The bitter sadness. Somehow they never met,
Poet and woman. Worse, say the stone skulls on the wall:
The wretched woman was no more than a screen,
The poet's plaintive anguish kneels at his own projections:
'O split-off self, I love you, you are so pure.'
So plangent, the exquisite art of self-torment.

At the end of his charming interpretation
The young man turns to brown skin and long fair hair:
I walk in the dampening long grass, aware of your moving thighs:

Poor Heine can go and bury himself and his self-defeating lies!

DAVID HOLBROOK

Schumann's Fantasy for Piano in C Major

In the country of longing, an endless road
loops the towns but never goes in.
C Major, the key this piece calls home,
is alluded to, circled again and again
(like the unreachable home in dreams)
but never arrived at until the end.
Strangely enough, you never mind;
you fall in love with the road instead.

C Major, affirming and uncomplex,
the first key any musician learns,
suitable for nursery rhymes
and for the stateliest anthems, seems
a brighter, more miraculous place
when it's encircled from outside.
I loved this piece at seventeen;
I thought I could reach C Major then.

Thirty years later, an old hand
at calling the country of longing home,
I prowl the place behind closed eyes
where long-remembered music lies.
Schumann's voice, flung like a dare,
summons the loves I coveted most,
pulls them from their prisons in time
and makes me view them yet again.

How beautiful their faces seem,
all these loves I never came near;
how miraculous from afar
the longed-for and unreachable towns;
how bright the eyes of the traveler
who rides the endless looping road
and through the darkening terrain
departs, returns, departs, returns.

MARCIA MENTER

The Maestro

'I'll portray you with flutes, oboes and harp.'
So Schumann to Clara. As I would you.

Now, in this front room of a tree-repeated street,
I practise mere stumbling tunes. But the maestro
behind me, in the mirror, my discreet double,
plays your music's parables flawlessly,
Schumann-like, strange and tragical and sweet.

DANNIE ABSE

R. Schumann

When down wind in Autumn's cool does drift
Schumann's music, the assertion and lament,
After tea time, it pleases men as much
As a gift
Given by a girl with all old birthright rent.

For on those floods and lights the regret comes
For all nobleness ever hurt, or truth denied,
Nor are those woods less mirrored than in lines
Old pageant's pride –
For darkling truth of earth never was better said.

And when that Schumann has told his mourning
There are not other words for any to say,
When his right and delight are restored, honour
They come to our day –
And we may drink his health till the pride of morning.

IVOR GURNEY

Tone Row

It was an obsession.
Before the music came
Schumann needed a few letters,
enough to make a coded message.
He would cull them
from a girl's name, a German town.

These were the seeds of sound
that would grow to a fantasy
or the chords of a caprice.
Here were the melodies
that spoke of dreams and childhood,
leaves from his album.

From his own name
he took four dancing notes
to make a carnival for his friends.
And how easily the music came,
to words scattered like confetti
over the songs of his marriage

before the long intervals of silence
when letters spelled terror;
before demons screamed a single note
as darkness fell and drove him naked
to the cold waters of the Rhine
and the asylum at Endernich.

BRIAN BIDDLE

FRANZ LISZT (1811–86)

Pianism

Fluid pianism. It was as if
               he sat down at a waterfall, it flowed
                        over his fingers and they wrestled
With the disappearing water; the piano's
               frame and strings reappeared
                        from moment to moment in the busy water
Then disappeared in a sudsy flux of brilliant
               current, or were marked across by some
                        new breeze of tributary torrent but
The sheerwhite style was creaselessly present:
               something in the speed; his hair flowed too
                        down to his shoulders and was a part
Of the music seen as well as heard,
               its sound matched the brilliance
                        of his hair-gloss and the white foam
Flowed over the piano's terraced ledges
               down his legs and over the stage
                        into the audience soaking them with Liszt.

PETER REDGROVE

Benediction

for Andrei Navrazov

'A state of pentatonic intoxication' –
So Alfred Brendel describes the listener's
Condition at the close of a piece by Liszt –

To gain which, so I think at daylight's end
(Chill glass in hand, and through another glass
The garden), one needn't actually be pissed.

'Master of the extended melodic line' –
Yes, after stubborn decades I bend the knee;
My old heart moved, though great with jealousy.

Intense, the fruit-trees' reds and indigos
Appear this year, the summer even more
Fleeting, because of flowing skies of grey.

Epoch when virtuosity must be
Transformed to sweet and melting simplicity.

ROY FULLER

A Music Lesson

Kröte's not well. His mood is bloody.
A pupil he can hardly stand
attacks a transcendental study.
—Lord, send me one real pianist.
Soul of a horse! He shapes her hand
and breathes apologies to Liszt.

'Reflect: in order to create
we must know how to. Think about
the balance between height and weight,
shoulder to fingertip; a hanging
bridge, resilient, reaching out
with firm supports. Let's have no banging!

'Playing begins inside your brain.
Music's much more than flesh and bone.
Relax, and listen. If you strain
your muscles *here* and *here* contract.
You get a stiff, unlovely tone.'
His pupil says, 'Is that a fact?'

She plays the passage louder, faster;
indeed deliberately tries
to infuriate her music master.
'The year that Liszt was born, a comet
blazed over European skies.'
'Am I to draw conclusions from it?

'And if so, what?' the tyro sneers.
– Cold heart, stiff hands. How to explain?
'When a new genius appears
it's like that fiery head of light
drawing us in its golden train.
Now, shall we try to get it right?

'Does it give you no pride to say
'My teacher's teacher learned from Liszt?'
Feel in your hands, before you play,
the body's marvellous architecture:
the muscles between hand and wrist
kept flexible; now try to picture

the finger forming, from the point
where it rests on the key, an arc
curving through every finger-joint,
supporting the whole arm's free weight.
Now the least effort makes its mark.
The instrument can sing.'
                              'I'm late,'

the pupil whines. The lesson's over.
The teacher pours himself a gin,
pats the piano like a lover
(– Dear mistress, we're alone once more).
Liszt, with his upper lip gone in,
beams from the cover of a score.

Abbé, forsooth! A toast to you,
old friend, old fiend in monkish dress.
I know you had your off days too.
At Schumann's, Clara said, you played
his work so badly once (confess!)
that only her good manners made

her sit in silence in that room.
– Have mercy on all pianists,
Architect of the world, of whom
I ask that I may live to see
Halley's Comet.
                    If God exists
then music is his love for me.

GWEN HARWOOD

GIUSEPPE VERDI (1813–1901)

Death at the Opera

Is this what death is like? I sit
Dressed elegantly in black and white, in an expensive seat,
Watching Violetta expire in Covent Garden.
How beautiful she is. As her voice lures me toward her death
The strings of the orchestra moisten my eyes with tears,
Though the tenor is too loud. Is this what death is like?
No one moves. Violetta coughs; stumbles toward the bed.
Twenty miles away in the country my father is dying.
Violetta catches at her throat. Let me repeat: my father
Is dying in a semi-detached house on a main road
Twenty miles off in the country. The skull is visible.

I do not want it to end. How exquisitely moving is death,
The approach to it. The lovers sob. Soon they will be wrenched apart.
How romantic it all is. Her hand is a white moth
Fluttering against the coverlet of the bed. The bones
Of my father's hands poke through his dry skin.
His eyes look into a vacancy of space. He spits into a cup.
In a few moments now Violetta will give up the ghost;
The doctor, the maid, the tenor who does not love her, will sob.
Almost, our hearts will stop beating. How refreshed we have been.
My father's clothes, too large for his shrunken frame,
Make him look like a parcel. Ah! The plush curtains are opening.

The applause! The applause! It drowns out the ugly noise
Of my father's choking and spitting. The bright lights
Glitter far more than the hundred watt bulb at home.
Dear Violetta! How she enjoys the flowers, like wreaths,
Showered for her own death. She gathers them to her.
We have avoided the coffin. I think that my father
Would like a box of good plain beech, being a man
From Buckinghamshire, a man of the country, a man of the soil.
I have seen my father, who is fond of animals, kill a cat
That was old and in pain with a blow from the edge of his palm.
He buried it in the garden, but I cannot remember its name.

Now the watchers are dispersing; the taxis drive away
Black in the black night. A huddle of people wait

Like mourners round the stage door. Is this what death is like?
For Violetta died after all. It is merely a ghost,
The voice gone, the beautiful dress removed, who steps in the rain.
Art, I conceive, is not so removed from life; for we look at death
Whether real or imagined, from an impossible distance
And somewhere a final curtain is always descending.
The critics are already phoning their obituaries to the papers.
I do not think God is concerned with such trivial matters
But, father, though there will be no applause, die well.

JOHN SMITH

Verdi at Eighty

1.

My brides are ravished away, are ravished away,
Two Leonoras, Gilda, Violetta,
One swaggering tenor has taken them,
One death seduced them to fever.

I have contrived a basso politics
To hunt him down, conspired
Through trio and quartette, strong situations,
Needled him on to my avenging sword.

2.

How shall a wicked, fat, old man be saved?
Connive with the women, incessant giggles and whispers.
He must be re-baptised in muddy water
And wash the district's dirty linen with him.
The wine will chirrup, an insect in old veins.
Ready then assume the sacrificial horns,
Grovel in terror before the Fairy Queen,
So that, our hope, lost lovers may re-join:
Nanetta find a tenor in the woods.
The festival will glow in basso nimbus of laughter.

MARTIN BELL

RICHARD WAGNER (1813–83)

Wagner

After the sick adventure and insolence
of steep soaring notes, heaven-lit,
the romantic convulsive fall and
fall to nuances of German black.

The suited orchestra inhabit the pit –
like the dead must be hidden.
Cthonic music must come back as if
bidden from the deeps of the earth.

Wagner, is this your dream or Wotan's?
An organ dismembered, a sexual shout,
scream and burn – climax of a candle-flame
blown out, more a woman's than a man's.

Genius with the soul of a vulture
your overgrown music is good for heroes,
for cheap Hollywood; yet there's something else,
something taciturn, almost remembered.

Outside the Hall even your statue, moon-blown,
stone-deaf, smells of the urn; and ghosts soaped
in moonlight weep. The streets of Germany
are clean, like the hands of Lady Macbeth.

And does your stern distinguished statue keep
vigil for another Fuhrer's return?
Some statues never awaken,
some never seem to sleep.

DANNIE ABSE

Brunhild

My father laid me in a ring
Of fire, and then like thunder rolled
Away, though I had been more close
To him than in his arms. He told
Me I should never see his face
Now he had voiced me like a song,

Made me a separate thing, no more
His warrior daughter but a woman.
But I do see his face, I see
It all the time. Though I am human
He can still rule. He promised me
That a brave man should break the fire,

A man he would approve of, no
Tentative weakling. He will have
My father's dominant beard and mighty
Shoulders, and instead of love
This obligation to be doughty.
I wait for the entrance of the hero

Dressed up in my father's fashion.
If I were free to love I would
Decide on someone thin and shaven.
But in the ring I lie like wood
Or soil, that cannot yield or even
Be raped except with his permission.

PATRICIA BEER

ANTON BRUCKNER (1824–96)

Anton Bruckner: Motet for Men's Choir
for Crispin Lewis

Sweat prickled the rehearsal-room walls
as the composer raged and spat.
'Too bloody *loud*. It's triple *p*.
And – God help us – you're *flat flat flat!*'

(The sixteen choristers sat in silence,
chins in, waiting to be dismissed.
They'd have an hour before the concert,
an hour after – at least they could get pissed.)

'Those final bars are a whisper, a dying fall.
They should barely reach me in the organ-loft.
Can't you get it into your turd-brains?
Not just soft, but softer than soft!'

*

Schnapps followed beer and hatched the plot
as the Angelus-bell began to chime:
at the finale, they would all open their mouths,
but no one would sing. The choir would mime.

*

Framed by organ-stops above the hushed nave,
the composer could not believe his ears:
a handful of notes – just this once, *his* notes –
joining the music of the spheres …

OLIVER REYNOLDS

May, 1945

As the Allied tanks trod Germany to shard
and no man had seen a fresh-pressed uniform
for six months, as the fire storm
bit out the core of Dresden yard by yard,

as farmers hid turnips for the after-war,
as cadets going to die passed Waffen SS
tearing identifications from their battledress,
the Russians only three days from the Brandenburger Tor –

in the very hell of sticks and blood and brick dust
as Germany the phoenix burned, the wraith
of History pursed its lips and spoke, thus:

To go with teeth and toes and human soap,
the radio will broadcast Bruckner's Eighth
so that good and evil may die in equal hope.

PETER PORTER

BEDŘICH SMETANA (1824–84)

Kateřina Smetana

He loved the past; that ancient heraldic grandeur,
Towers and armour glimmering in the mist;
Wind and hoof, castle and forest, fur
Nailed with ice, and flames against the snow.
The immortal river looping forests, rocks
And centuries. The saviour of myth;
Everything reminded him, keened in his head
Until it became a quickening and a faith,
A savage hope that blossomed into sound;
Until it became that waterfall of noise,
The jangle and unintelligible roar;
Until it became the inescapable,
The ceaseless whistle, the incessant E
That screamed in the homeland of his harmony.

I loved the past; when he ransacked the orchestra,
Shook from it stars and ancestors and meadows
Lit with flowers; he juggled with it, rode it,
Trapped it, whole, in string quartets, gave shape
To lives that always were and never were.
Now he is locked where none of us has been
And I can never go. The village dance
Is frozen, stars are stalled, and the huge howl
Of silence in his dreadful stare is all
That litters his staves. He will not touch my hair
Or hold my hand or wipe my tears. I am
The pain of lost music, the last glimmer
That proves the darkness running over fields.

NIGEL FORDE

JOHANNES BRAHMS (1833–97)

Brahms Peruses the Score of Siegfried

Enormous boots, thick-soled, elastic-sided,
Rest on a carpet shaggy as the pelt
         Of a mountain beast – perhaps
         Is precisely a mountain beast.

The chair adjoining, being unoccupied,
Reveals its antimacassar of scalloped lace
         Like the lower half
         Of a bikini of our day.

The frock-coat is disposed in folds as ample
As those of saints' robes in Renaissance painting:
         The pants, large cylinders
         Of a more recent art.

The background is a dark and shining wealth
Of gilt-tooled books, mahogany, and frames
         For photographs – for this,
         Eventually, no doubt.

The peering old man holds the little score so close
His white beard sweeps the page; but gives no sign
         That he perceives – or smells –
         Anything untoward.

He could not be expected to be thinking
That the legend of courage, kiss and sword arose
         From those atrocious Huns
         Who ruined an empire's comfort.

But how can he not be falling back aghast
At the chromatic spectrum of decay,
         Starting to destroy already
         His classical universe?

ROY FULLER

A Brahms Intermezzo

The heart is a minor artist
hiding behind a beard.
In middle age
the bloodstream becomes a hammock
slowing down for silence –
till then, this lullaby,
arpeggiated thunder
and the streams running
through Arcadia. I, too,
says the black-browed creature
am in this vale of sweetness,
my notes are added to eternity.

PETER PORTER

From *Brahms in Thun*

His hand moves over the page like a flock of birds
Seeking rest in snow, their tracks a relic
Of the enduring passage of a hunger
Across an infinite waste, a fragile heartbeat,
The Stockhorn, Niesen, and the Blümlisalp,
At once forbidding and familiar.

Quick, catch their flight … The hand continues to move,
The quavers swarm, the sheets fall from the piano,
The rhythms fight it out, the prey's in sight,
Crisp noble chords, the strings making decisions
That their invisible fingers lead them to,
The next idea that lies in wait for them.

The only respite is a dark Kaffee.
The ritual itself is stimulating:
His brass pot from Vienna with its spigot;
Its porcelain stand; the little burner moving
Its blue flame like a crocus underneath;
The grinding of the Mokka from Marseilles.

And a cigar, of course. And in its wreaths,
The music for a moment laid to rest,
He lives within the mood it has created:
And will one come again, will such a one?

And what on earth would happen if she did?
How to accommodate that bodied voice?

Herma, Herminche, Hermione-ohne-o!
Is it too late? Isn't the paradox
Just this: the one mistake committed is
The one that will transcend both fear and error
And in its act be no mistake at all?
And will one come again, will such a one?

Somewhere in his mind the names proceed
Like cases that have come to shape a law:
Clara, of course, Agathe, Julie, Lisl,
And all the singers of his Frauenchör
Whose voice and beauty caught his ear and eye,
Music's muses, music's priestesses.

They ring him round with their accusing looks.
He kneels before them in contrition, asking
Of song if the perfection of its moods
And of its utterance has power to
Redeem the soul of a defective man.
And song, as usual, has no sort of answer.

Nor does Kaffee. And nor do Frau Widmann's buttery
Plum pastries. Nor does the Wellingtonia.
Nor does that broad and energising vista
Across the lake where paddle-steamers ply,
The Stockhorn, Niesen, and the Blümlisalp,
Each reassuring as a reputation.

For there it is. The music must be written.
And Fräulein Spies will have her début in
Vienna. And Karlsgasse, num. 4 is only
An old bear's den, almost a hermit's cell.
And the Bernese summer, like every summer since
The beginning of the world, will soon be over.

And with the summer over, who can say
What may be found in the satchel of mysteries?
Wonderful Thun … The watchful fairy Schloss,
The midwife of his own late blossoming,
Herma, Herminche, Hermione-ohne-o,
The Trio, the Sonatas, and the Songs.

'Come, then, for one last time, for you will find me
Gone from a world that has no place for us.

But if you come, oh if you come, come soon!'
The instruments inscribe their own enticements
Upon the holy movement of a heart
Too long alone to know when it is teasing.

'It comes to me, this thing, whatever it is,
Like the spring flowers that steal upon the senses
And drift like scent away. Then comes the word
That holds it before my eye until it pales
Like the grey mist, and like a scent it dies.
Yet still a tear calls fragrance from its bud.'

That tear is music, emotion's memory,
And God forbid there should be story in it.
The good Herr Doktor with the forget-me-not eyes
Strides on, the emperor of a world of sound
So pure he scarcely sees that its grand truth
Is fatally wedded to the human voice.

JOHN FULLER

Concert, Southbank Centre, Spring 2006

Marin, and the London Phil
grab Brahms by the scruff of the neck
and hurl him
from one end of his Fourth to the other,
his feet never touch the ground,
(admit how you love this, Papa Brahms!) –

With her baton, Marin spins him
like a German dinner plate on a stick,
flicks him from violins to trumpets to drums
and back, *easy, easy!* to the violas
via French horns, bassoons, oboes and clarinets

She conducts him with her own electricity,
flexing every muscle in her body
under the folds of her well-cut grey suit,
red collar and shirt cuffs
ablaze for Brahms,
her arms, spine, hips, ankles
making one fluid harmonic –

With her beautiful back to us,
she's transforming the old warhorse
into an exuberant colt,
it's as if we've never heard the Fourth before,
music centred in a woman's knowledge-body,

and flying us high,
the QEH a shell through which the sea of a symphony
is pouring its tides and torrents –
till I feel, against my ear-lobes,
the tender bristles of the bushy grand-vizier beard of Brahms.

PENELOPE SHUTTLE

Sonata for Violin and Piano, Opus 78

If you listen often enough to a piece
it becomes a room, a series of rooms,
a home you know as well as the home
you're in and all the homes you've lost,
a desperately familiar place
that's also never the same place twice.

This piece starts with a lullaby,
processes through a funeral march
and ends on a rainy afternoon
when Brahms looks back, and back, and back
to songs he wrote as a younger man,
mourning a childhood that wasn't his.

I listened the first hundred times
to ride the rocking lullaby
and learn the pattern of the rain
by heart – it was all by heart back then.
Now I enter the piece to hear
the pattern of the listener.

All the hundreds of hearings dwell
behind a door in my body and mind
where all my younger and older selves
dance in a stately company,
taking their mutual joy in rain
and funeral march and lullaby.

MARCIA MENTER

CAMILLE SAINT-SAËNS (1835–1921)

Camille Saint-Saëns

The music came
As easy and as elegant as apples
For this, it seems, unloved, unloving man.

The nostrils of his enormous nose
Twitched, in scorn and anger
For the incompetent and the importunate.

The sugar softness of the wedding-cake
Was bait, to draw men down
Into the turning wheel, the grinding mill.

Women enslaved – were Omphale
And were Delilah; women betrayed their children.

And so he fled – to find the desolation
Of affluent hotel rooms, the icy desert
Of a continuing triumph,
And a State Funeral's final emptiness.

Only the animals
Were worthy to be loved, and sported
Through a perpetual carnival
In the lost playground of his innocence.

JOHN HEATH-STUBBS

'Softly Awakes My Heart …'

Saint-Saëns' aria
chosen by a man in Saudi Arabia
for his daughter in Ghana
(that version on His Master's Voice):
a Sunday morning World Service broadcast.

It brings a complex recall
of dusty velvet armchairs
a pile of records and the old victrola
net curtains faded and crisp
from sunlight through the dining room French window.

The mezzo-soprano
would smooth your mouth and eyes.
Your whole body calm except for
one hand turning on its wrist, accompanying.
I preferred a harsher music then.

RUTH FAINLIGHT

PYOTR TCHAIKOVSKY (1840–93)

The Butterfly Hears Tchaikovsky

Did it blunder in from the street?
Worse, imagine it reborn
among the platform flowers,
the first venture of delicate wings
wafting it straight to hell.
Our minds flooded with metaphor –
Francesca, Paolo, the manic winds
they're whirled in, all music
out of a soul in torment –
we watch that silky flier
lost in the glare, bewildered by
the shock of storming brass.
Flickering, it soars, dips,
traverses, its frail career
scribbled on art in a real
violence. When the applause breaks
it's gone – twitching perhaps
beside a player's foot, finished off
by the tuba's final blast,
the sumptuous crash of gong and cymbals.

RICHARD KELL

Old Usher

for Farès Moussa

I have
shouted Lights! in the foyer as the show begins

I have
opened and closed a million doors
Push and Pull stamping my palms

I have
woken with Good Evening on my lips

I have
ROH in moles over my left nipple

I have
Tchaikovsky as a heart-beat

I have
told ten thousand bladders
It's down the slope and on the right

I have
stood at the bottom of Floral Hall stairs
with Peter Bramley at the top
tapping the metal hand-rail with his ring
to annoy me

I have
bent my head to complaints about the row in front
the big hair-do, the change-jingler, those who snore or smell

I have
turned a blind eye, a deaf ear, and a stopped nostril

I have
opened and closed a million doors
Push and Pull stamping my palms

I have
waited in the wings to present flowers
cygnets wafting past me in a crush of tutus
each back tight with the cordage of muscle

I have
sold ices with Susie Boyle

I have
passed the black-and-white monitor at Stage Door
and felt proud to see Haitink in the pit
a bottled homunculus preserved in music

I have
opened my locker on a vista of dirty shirts

I have
killed a moth for Monica Mason
It wants to *settle* on me!
she who once danced her death in the *Rite*
now frightened of millimetres of flutter

I have
Tchaikovsky as a heart-beat

I have
bassoons and strings planned for my last-act death
the weightless *pas-de-chat*
lifting me out of this ninth life
into the proscenium's eternal gold

I have
perfected my farewell
a final turning-out of the pockets
as I rise and vanish into air
swirling with the confetti of ticket-stubs

I have
shouted Lights! as the show begins

I have

OLIVER REYNOLDS

ANTONÍN DVOŘÁK (1841–1904)

Music Student, First Violinist
(in the Dvořák D Minor Symphony)

Anton, all the black notes of your symphony
Have swarmed into this girl's allegro hair.
Only the sluggard breves and minims stay
Trapped by the bars of the conductor's score.

Pours frozen from her crown's simple motif
A black cascade of glistening counterpoint
To where my gladly martyred eyes receive
Ten thousand quavers' barbed and startling points,
Where the taut canvas chairback lets it go.

So near, I could imprison with my hand
The tempting weight of that polyphony,
Tug her bent head back from the weaving bow.
There is a melody in each separate strand,
Had I a chance to study its great score;
Your temporal genius rendered spatially.

It is too short, this timeless hour. The time
To plumb its currents, ponder how it weaves
From the home minor to a major key
And brings it back, find if it joys or grieves
In its own ponderings of its own shut score,
Cannot be measured by the metronome,
Or clock, or pulse, or carbon in the rocks.

I catch its shampoo's faintly lurking theme
And sense the recent crisis – she attacked
Lacklustre strands with demons in her hands.
All was dismay – will it be right in time?
She hacked its knots before the fire. Tonight
The whole performance is in place, exact;
Blue-hazed with static electricity.
Her soul's in music, music in her hair.

Symphony of her darkest attribute.
She'll wrap it in a scarf, and disappear.

A tube will hold her and her buried stream.
Since art is less than life, agree
That I do right, amidst the coughs, to hear
No music but its waist-long cataract.
She will express you just as passionately
When all the white notes of your symphony,
Unlike the black notes dead within the score,
In the rich coda of the major key
Have swarmed into this girl's adagio hair.

D. M. THOMAS

Sycamore

The sycamore stumps survived the deadliest gales
To put out new growth, leaves sticky with honeydew
And just enough white wood to make a violin.

This was a way of mending the phonograph record
Broken by the unknown soldier before the Somme
(Fritz Kreisler playing Dvořák's 'Humoresque').

The notes of music twirled like sycamore wings
From farmhouse-sheltering-and-dairy-cooling branches
And carried to all corners of the battlefield.

MICHAEL LONGLEY

ARTHUR SULLIVAN (1842–1900)

A Quartet
(The Mikado *at Cambridge*)

Four singers with a Delphic seriousness
In harmony's kind problem play their part,
And I, who see and hear, think they express
Nature's best gift, the calm delight of art.
The fourfold music takes its twining ways,
And like a rich spring underwood embowers
Their careful theme, which from the tonal maze
Sudden as a nightingale all bright outflowers
When that dark lady bids a madrigal.
O sweet content, reward in deed, release
Of spirit here in imperfection shut;
Symmetry's answer given without a 'but';
Deep-moved I mark their choral masterpiece,
Their union in each swell and dying fall.

EDMUND BLUNDEN

EDVARD GRIEG (1843–1907)

For the Grieg Centenary

The fells are jagged in the shining air; the wind
Sharpens itself like a knife on the rough edges:
The sky is blue as ice, and clouds from the sea
   Splinter above the land
And drive against the rocks in thin steel wedges.

This of all England is the place to remember Grieg:
Here where the Norsemen foraged down the dales,
Crossing the sea with the migrant redwing,
   Thieving heifer and yow and teg,
Leaving their names scotched on the flanks of the hills.

Leaving also the crackling northern tongues,
The dialect crisp with the click of the wind
In the thorns of a wintry dyke,
   So that Solveig sings
In the words which bind the homes of Cumberland.

Therefore let Solveig sing in the western dales
When the frost is on the pikes, and the raven builds again
Its nest in February; let Crinkle Crags
   Be thumped by the humpbacked trolls,
And the voice of Grieg ring loud through the sound of the sea
   and the rain.

NORMAN NICHOLSON

GABRIEL FAURÉ (1845–1924)

Fauré

Take me aboard your barque, where the valuable water
  Mirrors the perfect passage of the dove.
Over the glittering gulf the sun burns whiter
  The charts of envy and the reefs of love.

Lost in the frosty light the desperate hunter
  Hurls his black horn-note on the wrecked château
Where in despair the signalman of winter
  Winds on its walls the flashing flags of snow.

I see (captured my caravel) the stolen city
  Falling like Falcon to the cunning bay.
The holy sea, unmerciful and mighty,
  Strides with the tide its penance all the day.

Fling like a king your coin on the clear passage
  Bribing the sea-guard and the stumbling gun.
On the salt lawn scribble your last message
  Rallying the rout of ice on the storming sun.

CHARLES CAUSLEY

Fauré in Paris, 1924

Nearing eighty, Fauré has found the end
of sound. He never would have guessed
it had so much to do with the Mediterranean
light of childhood, or lake breezes swirling
all summer at Savoy, and so little to do
with music growing quieter everywhere
but in his mind. He is relieved to hear
the garbled edge of what had been music,
his torment for twenty years, fading at last
to silence. If only his breath would follow!

He believes he is finished with the flesh,
his face now thin and delicate as a lost note
dissolving in air, his body closing in

on itself, the discordant coda to a life
of elegance and song. He would become
spirit instead, simple and radiant at the level
of pure grace, diaphanous against nightfall.
He hoards his bare, inner music and must
force himself to reduce it to notes on a page.

Alone, deaf to street noise below, the call
of birds above, seeing the Paris sky glazed
with loud sunlight, he feels wrapped
in melody's softest shroud. It is exquisite,
as he always knew it must be, and almost
liquid in the way it lifts him toward the clouds.

FLOYD SKLOOT

Après Un Rêve

In my Mother's Day siesta
I dreamed
a poet called me on the phone –

'I can't talk long, Penny,'
he said,
'there's a guy staying with me

who's very unhappy,
he's waited weeks for his girlfriend
to call, so he doesn't like me

using the phone,
but listen' –

Now he must be holding the phone
out to the room
as the unhappy guy plays the piano and sings –

Après Un Rêve –
far-off and faint, the most beautiful rendition
I've ever heard,

so beautiful that when he's done,
I just put down the phone in wonder
without a word

to the poet or his friend the singer.

PENELOPE SHUTTLE

LEOŠ JANÁČEK (1854–1928)

Diary of One Who Disappeared
Janáček JW 5/12

This piece for solo voice
and piano: both have turned
their backs to the window
I unlocked earlier
to let a cool breeze in
for this young audience
as they follow the music
up and down. The window
opens onto an alley
that travels a few yards
to a murmur of traffic
on Brent Street. Some of us
(the least attentive)
catch sight of shoppers
strolling past or pick out
scraps of passing talk
till a grey, untidy head
comes to a halt outside.
Thin-lipped, she blankly
stares at neither singer
nor seated pianist …
Nor does she fix her gaze
on faces around the room.
Outside, a breath of wind
stirs, then slips across
the sill to lift a sheet
of music from its stand.
Just in time, the singer's
quick professional hand
sets it back in place.
And still, her steady head
in silence is inclined
to the kind of pleasures
sad music affords. Then
'Bravo!' in a hoarse,
thick accent she calls,
as soon sinks from sight,

reappears – her raised hand
crossing the window-sill –
she introduces a yellow
flower she has plucked
from the foot of the wall.
She calls again 'Bravo!'
and my eyes are shut
to see desolate streets,
neighbourhoods failed,
find kicked-in doorways
left open to the rain,
track her disappeared
into camps and ditches,
the lucky scattering
where their journey slows
to this pedal-note of
idling cars, these brown,
pallid and olive faces,
this sunlit afternoon
in this English town,
these peremptory gifts
from one already gone.

MARTYN CRUCEFIX

On a Farm Track, Northumberland

It saw us coming, our barn owl,
took off in a shock
of buff-white splayed feathers
into the wood, into the mist,
into our memory,

whereas Leoš Janáček,
on that overgrown path of his
observed, for long enough, one
that, by the grace of his music,
has not flown away and never will.

Strange, how he caught what he caught
on the touch of a piano
that touches something, leaves me

wondering what of the barn owl's being
made him say it that way.

Ours wouldn't sound like his.
If I could make music of it
I wouldn't choose piano, but what?
Too obvious to mimic the rocks
singing water through Harthope Burn,

small rain minutely percussive
on leaf, bracken, grass, ground;
ewes, alert to our footfall, warning
lambs grown beyond their nurturing;
rooks dancing cracked and feathered air.

Walking this northern shadowed land,
battled from iron-age
through Roman, Anglo-Saxon, Viking,
in what fear, greed, need,
for what loss or gain,

I would draw the bow,
not in warfare, but in a slow adagio
on violin strings, unsettling the air
in harmony with the silence
of those thick-fledged wings.

HELEN ASHLEY

EDWARD ELGAR (1857–1934)

The Nightingale Broadcasts

Beatrice Harrison, who lived in a remote house in woodland
  south of Oxted, Surrey, was a distinguished cellist.
She was thirty-one when she tried to persuade Lord Reith to sanction
  the BBC's recording, to be broadcast live, of a tryst

she was planning in her garden, with nightingales
  in a copse, accompanied by herself on the cello
playing Elgar, whose favourite soloist she was – if it happened,
  this would be the first ever live outdoor radio

broadcast. In May 1923, on a bench in a sea of bluebells,
  she'd been playing 'Chant Hindou' by Rimsky-Korsakov
when a nightingale had swollen into song 'in thirds,
  and always in tune' with her, from deep in a nearby grove.

It was the following spring, while making her broadcasting debut
  as soloist in Elgar's Cello Concerto with Elgar
conducting, that she'd first hit upon the idea of nightingales singing
  for the nation. Lord Reith supposed they'd be real prima

donnas – costly and unpredictable – and he was also chary
  of packaging nature, of making birdsong 'second-hand'.
But Miss Harrison pleaded the case of the poor – all those
  without motorcars, in cities and the north of England.

A rehearsal went well. The broadcast, planned for 19th May,
  would interrupt the Savoy Orpheans' Saturday night dance
music programme just as the Oxted nightingales started
  their evening crescendo. What a performance! –

the summerhouse filled with amplifiers, engineers swarming
  in the undergrowth. Miss Harrison played in a ditch –
Elgar, Dvořák, 'Danny Boy'. Silence. Then, fifteen minutes before
  the station went off the air, a nightingale cadenza, which

gargled and trilled from the oak leaves, flowered through
  a million radios and crystal sets, some of them outdoors,
themselves setting off nightingales, or building in the night air
  a city of song in alien habitats – cornfields, moors,

mountains, housing. For twelve years the BBC broadcast
  Miss Harrison's nightingale concerts (one of them, set up near
a pond, featuring a chorus of frogs). After she moved house,
  the birds were recorded solo, not every year

but certainly in 1942, when engineers captured a nightingale
  outsung but not silenced by a fleet of Lancasters
droning overhead, the first of the 'thousand bomber' raids,
  targeting Cologne, archived though never broadcast.

The RAF had discovered that two out of three bombs dropped
  in night raids on Germany had missed their aim
by more than five miles. Area bombing would be much more accurate.
  In the event, both sides turned out to have the same

problem: the average number of days at work lost
  through bombing was only five. Although often
workers' homes were destroyed, morale stayed high: men and women
  still worked, for their country and their distant children.

ROBERT SAXTON

To the City of Worcester

Little I remember about Her that I care for,
Being too great a lover of my own City, and
Longing for Westgate Street, and the coloured great Choir.
The Cotswolds I knew and the book shops and streets I knew.
But there in the Festival time, a kind lady of years
Housed me, and fed me as she thought boys should be fed.
I sang *Gerontius* and saw brown Severn strand;
Bought *Sapphic Ode* of Brahms, and knew Elgar was born,
To whose thought Norway and Rome were brought,
And the Christian worship meditated un-exalted.
I hero worshipper, full of *Gerontius* and the *Beatitudes*
Saw himself stand with serious slender attitudes
To be as rapt in what he had done as anyone
Of all the attentive Chorus, or all-skilled Band.
To see a live Hero not four yards ahead …

But still the chief thought of that City is yet the decorated
Infinite lines of ornament that so irritated
My Gloucester-clean mind for fine plainness.

And the damned Cathedral organ that always broke
Down when least looked for, and not in any joke.
And the overeating the queen kind hostess did force
On me, all ignorant of stresses or strains – or the comfort of space.

IVOR GURNEY

The Dream of Edward Elgar

There's a story the composer
used to tell. About weeks
in the middle of a hard winter
when insomnia, silence, and sickness
were the only prayers he could hear.
And about the evening he returned to work

until *The Dream of Gerontius* was complete,
after hearing voices outside,
and, in a downpour of sleet,
helping a neighbour bind
a blizzard of sheep
away from darkness and the road.

In a letter to a friend
some years later, he seemed
moved by the ease of it all,
by the passing sounds and the ease
with which each note fell,
almost taken to be real.

He said he thought the simple
movement was the same
as that from night-blindness to understanding shapes.
As each time, finished in the drawing-room,
he would blow against a lamp
and find himself blindfolded in a pallid gloom.

Until the last shapes of his age
separated, and night snowed
against the mirror, the cream drapes,
the notepaper, the piano,
the lampshade,
the mantelpiece, the bay window.

CONOR O'CALLAGHAN

GIACOMO PUCCINI (1858–1924)

Libretto

Libretto. That's the first Italian word
  she wants to teach me: 'little book.'
This afternoon (but why are we alone?
  Were Daddy and my brothers gone
all day, or has memory with its flair
  for simple compositions air-
brushed them from the shot?) she's set aside
  just for the two of us, and a lesson.

On an ivory silk couch that doesn't fit
  the life she's given in Detroit,
we gaze across the living room at the tall
  'European' drapes she's sewn
herself: a work of secret weights and tiers,
  hung after cursing at her own
mother's machine. She lets the needle fall
  onto the record's edge; then turns

to pull a hidden cord, and the curtain rises
  on Puccini's strings and our front view
of shut two-car garages, built for new
  marriages constructed since the war.
Well, not so new. It's 1962
  and though I'm only eight, I know
that with two cars, people can separate.
  He went away; he came back for more

operatic scenes heard through the wall
  as if through a foreign language. Muffled
fury and accusation, percussive sobs:
  they aren't happy. Who couldn't tell
without the words? *Libretto.* On my knees
  the English text, the Italian on hers,
and a thrill so loud the coffee table throbs.
  I'm following her finger as

we're looping to a phrase already sung
  or reading four lines at a time
of people interrupting and just plain
  not listening, and yet the burden
of the words is simple: Butterfly must die.
  Pinkerton will betray her, though the theme

rippling above him like a hoisted flag
  is The Star-Spangled Banner. Mother, why

would a Japanese and an American
  sing Italian at each other?
Why would he get married and not stay?
  And have a child he'd leave to wait
with the mother by the screen with her telescope
  for the ship of hope? Why, if he knew
it wouldn't last, did he come back to Japan?
  – But I'm not asking her. *That's men*

is her tacit, bitter answer; was always half
  her lesson plan. *O say, can you see …*
yes, now I can. Your dagger's at the throat
  and yet I feel no rage; as tears
stream down our faces onto facing pages
  fluttering like wings, I see you meant
like Butterfly to tie a blindfold over
  a loved child's eyes: the saving veil of Art.

For it is only a story. When the curtain
  drops, our pity modulates
to relief she isn't us, and what's in store
  for you, divorce and lonely death,
remains distant. We have our nights to come
  of operas to dress up for,
our silly jokes, our shopping, days at home
  when nothing is very wrong and in my chair

I read some tragedy in comfort, even
  a half-shamed joy. You gave me that –
my poor, dear parents, younger then than I
  am now; with a stagestruck, helpless wish
that it wouldn't hurt and that it would, you made
  me press my ear against the wall
for stories that kept me near and far,
  and because the hurt was beautiful

even to try to write them; to find that living
  by stories is itself a life.
Forgive whatever artifice lies
  in my turning you into characters
in my own libretto – one sorry hand
  hovering above the quicksand
of a turntable in a house in Detroit
  I can't go back to otherwise.

MARY JO SALTER

Puccini

In his little book of ideas Signor Puccini
drew pictures of Paris,
the Wild West, the Orient.

Whatever he heard
– applause, the waves, the rustle of silk –
he turned into a chord for strings.

He kept his hair lacquered
and from under the brim of his hat
looked for consolation

sometimes in the Red Light District,
sometimes in the chorus and arias
of music that tore his heart out.

GERARD SMYTH

HUGO WOLF (1860–1903)

Hugo Wolf at Traunkirchen

The water was still in mourning,
preserving more than a reflection
of his tormented face.

Bone, flesh and blood fell like a star,
his life one rage too far
to bear another gift.

The lake was then unwilling to accept
one for whom joy was spent,
his mind burnt out.

Was it a kindness to haul him back
to his insanity, speechless
and paralysed?

Here was a man, whose anger could be roused
by a cricket chirping in his room,
made dumb as the moon.

We rowed across his dark, aborted grave
and felt the shadows cling
like oil-slicks to our bow.

EDWARD STOREY

GUSTAV MAHLER (1860–1911)

From *Her Vertical Smile*

I

Arms uplifted on the podium,
   the left hand dangling tyrannical;
aetat fünfzig;

the stance flat footed;
   the face a fragile axe,
hard and acid, rapt.

Everything a man can do,
   and more, is done,
the sparse hair thrown back,

the white cuffs flaring,
   the ivory baton flourished
and driven deep.

He sports a little paunch
   but this, in its boxy waistcoat,
merely emphasizes the force of will

we find everywhere
   in his strange work:
the readiness to embrace risk,

tedium, the ignoble,
   to try anything ten times
if so the excessive matter can be settled.

(We have waltzed a while with Disaster,
   coat tails twirling along the precipice,
and She is charmed senseless,

Her harmonies collapse
   at a touch.) Only a double drum
is beating: two hearts coupled.

There is an overpowering tinkle;
    a pregnant hush.
Masterful yet sensitive

his baton explores
    her core of peace,
every rhythm drained

into nothing, the nothingness
    adjusting toward
a new readiness.

From his captive hearers
    (though we can scarcely
contain ourselves)

not a cough,
    not a shuffle,
his stance pivotal

above the excited young
    clustered around him
in all our promise,

focused with shining faces
    on the place of measurement itself,
pointing, like children.

Not a stir,
    not a breath,
there at the heart of old Vienna.

THOMAS KINSELLA

Das Lied von der Erde

Roses have fallen, the flesh has lost its tune,
the sound of flutes silvers a chilling moon;
the glint of wine has soured upon the tongue;
riderless now the horsing seasons come;
gone are the firm of limb whose laughter kissed
the morning air with hope, the longing dusk
with traced desires. Now, as the scent of musk
fingers old graveyards, moulders thought from books,
and breathes its doubt on well-remembered looks,
Ewig ... the music sighs, and brings us near
the silence those it folds on never hear.

MAURICE LINDSAY

Kindertotenlieder

There can be no songs for dead children
Near the crazy circle of explosions,
The splintering tangent of the ricochet,

No songs for the children who have become
My unrestricted tenants, fingerprints
Everywhere, teethmarks on this and that.

MICHAEL LONGLEY

FREDERICK DELIUS (1862–1934)

Delius & Fenby

*To be a genius, as this man plainly was, and have something beautiful in you
and not be able to rid yourself of it because you could no longer see your score
paper and no longer hold your pen – well, the thought was unbearable!*

Eric Fenby, Delius As I Knew Him

Always toward sunset Delius grew
restless and uneasy in his carriage
chair, raving at the pain in his legs,
flicking his long tapering fingers
as though stating a theme on the air.
His proud head, pale as marble,
began to wobble no matter the effort
to hold it still. He demanded a thick
rug for warmth. He demanded a thin rug
for comfort, then demanded that no
rug touch him, all the time wanting
me to read one more story aloud
like a child refusing to go to bed.

Delius required that everything
be just so. His bean and barley
soup must be salted in the pot
and served piping hot. No rattling
cups or clattering spoons at table,
where chitchat lashed him to fury.
After dinner, one cigar and a slow
push up the Marlotte road in silence,
when even the neighbor's great Alsatians
walked hushed beside us. Saturdays
we could play only Sir Thomas Beecham's
records of Delius on the gramophone
in the quiet of his music room.

One morning in the faded garden
where Delius sat beneath the elder
tree, I could see that he was angry
with me. Tossing his head from side
to side, he champed and glared
toward the rising sun, clearing
his throat *fortissimo*. At night

a melody had come on the verge
of sleep, making him weep to be
hearing new music leap in his mind
again. But I overslept beneath
the full-sized face of mad Strindberg
by Munch, dreaming myself south
to Paris amidst a wild summer storm,
surrounded by young friends in good
health, rain playing a sudden cadenza
on the swollen Somme, and the thunder
in E-Flat. I wanted tea.

My hair still damp, my face creased
by sleep, I took up paper and pen
without a word. I sat cross-legged
on the grass wondering whether Delius
would sing to me. Would he call out
the notes and their time-values?
At last I was to do what I had come
from Scarborough to do and free him
of the music. He threw his head
back like a wild horse in flight
and neighed toneless to the sky.
'Hold it!' he said, causing me
to drop my pen, then he bayed
toward heaven again. I heard
neither words nor notes, only
a shapeless cry. He could not
bring forth the tune he heard!
Dazed, all I could say was
'Delius, what key is it in?'
'A minor, Fenby, don't be slow.'

Fingers inky, spectacles blurred
by tears, I confess being blind
as Delius himself when I groped
for the sanctuary of his porch.
Of course, in time we learned
to bring forth his music, imagining
ourselves on cliffs in the heather
looking out over the sea, knowing
chords in the high strings were
a clear sky. But I shall never
forget Delius, a shrunken relic,
mouth opened in anguish, gripped
by the awful beauty inside him.

FLOYD SKLOOT

CLAUDE DEBUSSY (1862–1918)

The Submerged Cathedral

(In memory of Phyllis Robinson)

*I have made mysterious nature my religion … to feel the supreme
and moving beauty of the spectacle to which Nature invites
her ephemeral guests, that is what I call prayer.*

CLAUDE DEBUSSY

It's an hour before the dawn of rock 'n' roll:
Music has not so far been made flesh –
Or not for a working-class girl of thirteen.
And then I watch you play, star graduate
Of James Ching and the Matthay School,
Your technique so physical, so lavish,
I'd call it, now, *l'écriture féminine*
For pianists: but in 1958
All I know is that you are what you're playing –
You're playing *La Cathédrale Engloutie.*

A camera's drawn to the concert pianist's hands,
Caressing octaves, palely capering –
Sunday *Palladium* stuff, with Russ Conway
Or Winifred Atwell (coos from the mums and dads),
To be filed under my new word: *Philistine.*
This is art so deep it's industry:
Music as white-water, which your spine
Channels, springing arms transform. That's how
You lift and tumble these ton-weights of bell power:
I watch you, not your hands. I watch the sea,

Out of my depth, though, like *La Cathédrale.*
I mean all this to last – the eight hours' practice
Each day, hopeless devotion – and it does –
In other contexts. Oh, I bury it,
Music, and you, and all the pain of childhood,
But lumber back like a medieval builder
With washed-up stones (some good stone, too) and prayers,
To raise another heaven-touching marvel
On the same flood-site, watch another tide
Swagger in and demolish every bit.

After the last wreck, when I'd declared
The end of building-works on any coast,
Strange bells began to ring for me, the tone
Rubbed ordinary by forty years, but true:
Ghostly but not damned. What if the ghost
Wryly sang, 'Promises, promises?'
It was a gentle challenge, after all.
The sacred stones were myth. The tide that reared
So vengefully, hauled by the same moon,
Was myth. Not so, my common ground with you.

How we talk up 'the generation gap',
Break our necks in it, and never find
The friendly criss-cross trails of co-existence –
That gift which is to pause at one epoch,
The people of one earth. Yes, the years wear us …
But may all years be worn as you wore yours
That day we met, with teacherly compassion,
Because the body knows when the brighter mind
Rejects it, sulks like an untuned piano:
You lived in yours (it knew) like the luckiest girls.

It's hard, though, for the tired cells to sightread
Their last prélude, fingers twisting palm-ward,
In search of rarer ivory, their guiding
Beat a laggard stone-deaf walking-stick.
Like Schubert's songs, off in another key
Before we can say 'swan', you were elsewhere:
And elsewhere, in a room nearby, your music.
I'd wanted you to play. I let that go.
You counted off your new pursuits, confiding
'I love the sea. I love to watch *la mer*!'

On Portrush Strand I watch it too, engrossed
Like a child beside a piano, half aware
That this, whatever 'this' may be, won't keep,
The waves themselves won't keep. But someone plays
Debussy. Something rescues the white horses
You're not admiring now – not from these shores,
And makes them flesh, as music was, for me,
An hour before the dawn of rock 'n' roll
When you, star graduate of the Matthay School,
Lifted the great bells out of the sea.

CAROL RUMENS

RICHARD STRAUSS (1864–1949)

Covent Garden in the Sixties

Here where bridges to the past
may be trodden by a team of cheating gods
or carry the companionable dead
back to life from their long overcast
empyrean, we sat, not quite at odds
with one another, staring ahead
at the usual muddle on the stage.
Maestro Solti's dome, tympanum
of a Straussian downbeat, bobbed
above the pit. Two ladies of uncertain age,
tiara'd, satin'd, shifted bum to bum
through three long acts, happily hob-nobbed
with their kind in intervals
and made our evening comic at the end –
one asked, 'What did you make of it?'
'Too long, too loud.' That memory annuls
for me the real pain the music sends
straight to my slow conscience: I admit
that marriage and the seed of life need Strauss
to fill them with appropriate harmony.
Human creatures worsen in the light
and cannot make a temple of a house;
the birds which clamour in the family tree
are vultures and not falcons; every night
the court of dreams must pass its sentence
while scores and books and pictures rush
to judgment on their makers – why else
come where the trials of gods commence,
where Neo-Babylonian tiers of plush
pretend they wait on pleasure and our hells
and heavens are strictest shuntings of the air.
I know we courted love and couldn't believe
that it had come and then that it had gone –
years later in a park I saw a pair
of birds like us – she streamed, he had to weave,
hopalong goose who thought himself a swan.

PETER PORTER

Serenade

It was after the Somme, our line was quieter,
Wires mended, neither side daring attacker
Or aggressor to be – the guns equal, the wires a thick hedge,
When there sounded, (O past days for ever confounded!)
The tune of Schubert which belonged to days mathematical,
Effort of spirit bearing fruit worthy, actual.
The gramophone for an hour was my quiet's mocker,
Until I cried, 'Give us *Heldenleben, Heldenleben.*'
The Gloucesters cried out 'Strauss is our favourite *wir haben
Sich geliebt*'. So silence fell, Aubers front slept,
And the sentries an unsentimental silence kept.
True, the size of the rum ration was still a shocker
But at last over Aubers the majesty of the dawn's veil swept.

IVOR GURNEY

Indian Summer

This day is wholly unsullied,
golden and beneficent. I sit
in my recommissioned deck-chair
by the garden path. From a cerulean sky
the sun's unwinking stare
fixes the world in stasis, warm and somnolent.
This is the weather of myth.
Not a rumour of air
stirs in the limp laburnum, or anywhere;
all is so still and soundless you could hear
the wing-beat of a moth,
except that from my open window drift
faint sounds of Strauss's *Tod und Verklärung*
and yet more faintly, now and then, is heard,
closer, underneath my hand,
dry whisper of a turning page
as I peruse, with awful delectation,
The Oxford Book of Death.

VERNON SCANNELL

JEAN SIBELIUS (1865–1957)

Sibelius

The forests discern him,

the forests of idle turbulent rain,

whose horses, bridled, barely,

whose chariots, burn.

GILLIAN ALLNUTT

Barkbröd

for Michael Mott

I used to think of him as Väinämöinen – seer, demigod.
I told him to his face once, when flushed with wine.
He smiled his sour smile and called me 'cheesemonger'.

Last week he told me that an elk had stamped his lawn.
(Of course reindeer milk gives the best of gamey cheeses.)
I told him his 'Kullervo' called all creatures home.

I went with Birgit to Helsinki for his symphony.
What I heard there was a growling. We took the tailor, Hirn,
who singled out the culprits: bassoon and double bass.

Someone said this new work sounded 'mountainous'.
'Barkbröd', Hirn said. 'Like the mix of grain and tree bark
which kept our ancestors alive'. Others took the likeness up.

"'Austere', 'introspective', 'spare'?" the maestro sneered
when I told him that his Fourth brought Barkbröd to mind.
He flapped his hands about as if such compliments were flies.

I took exception to the gesture. Flies in my shop!
Then he turned on our tutunmaa, a perfectly pale yellow,
and declared it 'off'. I gestured towards the door.

'Allow me,' I said, 'to know and nurse my own cheeses'.
(He patronised me, he once said, for my turn of phrase.
'It's just as Finnish as your symphonies,' I replied.)

Not content, he singled out my juustoleipä for abuse.
To him it might as well have been old gammalost
that nourished Norsemen on their long sea trips.

I've thought of him as one of our forefathers since,
his fine hands clutching rough dark rye barkbread.
Yes, he would yearn then for my 'elemental' cheeses.

TONY ROBERTS

Sibelius's Fifth Symphony in the Dead of Winter

When I hear that theme rising from nowhere,
naming the home key, stating the fact
of the home key as though no other truth
existed: *Do. Sol. Do. Ti. Sol.*
I am certain as of nothing else
that certainty is possible.
Here it is, thank god, thank god,
I knew it was someplace. Here it is.

Every time the theme appears
rising through chatter innocent
or pernicious, slipping into the ear
as a loved one's hand slips into yours,
the blessed certainty returns,
the sense of home, even when the key
is corrupted and the harmonies veer
into the muddy and sinister.

Pry apart the music's layers –
order and chaos, bleakness and light
jammed together as in life –
plot the course of the theme and learn

the crystalline logic driving it.
Nothing kills the mystery.
There is something carrying on.
There is something carrying me.

Rising through the ominous days
how spare and matter-of-fact it is
like the ticking of a watch
marking the moment quietly,
like the naming of a key
where there is no belief in keys,
like the turning of the ear
toward the theme that must be heard.

MARCIA MENTER

From *The Cold Musician*

December dawn, moon and morning star are alone.
Shadows of bare twigs on white walls hardly move.

Luonnotar – this music is aeons colder
than suburban frost that makes children hurry.
How cold was creation? Only the cold survive
and she survived, waiting for motherhood.
Her desire must have been harder than ice.

A postcard from Uppsala: trees rigid crystal
and cathedral spire unwavering in its aim.
Heaven is blue for a few hours and always cold.
The will to keep pointing like that must be harder than stone.

ROBIN FULTON MACPHERSON

ERIK SATIE (1866–1925)

Erik Satie and the Blackbird

on listening to Satie's 'Vexations' played from noon to dawn by a relay of pianists in Salem Chapel, Hay-on-Wye

The blackbird sings
for eighteen hours
with a bead of rain
in its throat.
First notes at first light.
Four in the morning
and he'll be there
with his mouth full of gold.

The piano crosses an ocean
on one wing,
noon to midnight
and through to dawn.
This is the nightshift,
you and the rain
and the pianist awake,
navigating the small hours.

While the blackbird sleeps
under a dark wing,
the town breathing,
the wash of a car on a wet street,
the world turns over
in the dark. The sleepless
travel on. They know by heart
their own refrains.

The pianist doesn't turn the page.
Just back to the top
where music collects
opening its throat to the rain,
and somewhere two bells
count down the hours
towards first light, landfall,
the downpour of a blackbird singing.

GILLIAN CLARKE

AMY BEACH (1867–1944)

The Composer Amy Beach

Phenomenally gifted as a child, she soon acquired a reputation as a piano virtuoso, but this was later superseded by a recognition of her accomplishments as a composer. She was the first composer in America to write a symphony of importance.

Percy A. Scholes, *The Oxford Companion to Music*

I

Amy, we must put a stop to this.
What is it Calvin tells us? *Take from a child*
That thing he loves most.
Since you could toddle you've played
Every song we've sung you.
We do this for your own dear sake.

II

We could never make out how Mrs Cheney
Could be that cruel. But, in any case,
There was no stopping the child.
Without her piano she took to playing
The stairs – knelt on the bottom one,
Played her tunes on the next.
Stood her music on the one above.
She was always to be found there; always.
One day a visitor called and had words
With Mrs Cheney. We didn't hear
What was said, but from that day on
Amy played piano all the time.

III

I have been the most fortunate of women,
With loving parents, my fine husband, my music.
They said that when I was small I mastered Chopin
Even though my hands were the hands of an infant.
But somehow, according to Mother, I knew
Which of the notes it was best to leave unplayed.
My concerts made Boston the focus of the world.
I adored making music; I was adored.

114

In the contract I signed on my marriage to Doctor Beach
Was a clause that said I would cease to play in public.
Young women ask me how did that feel?
I don't remember. They find it hard to believe.
But I thank God daily for it now;
For guiding me down this road.

FRANCES NAGLE

RALPH VAUGHAN WILLIAMS (1872–1958)

The Death Has Occurred ...

… of Ralph Vaughan Williams. Sad August 1958:
my Cambridge is over; and now, more loved
than either grandfather, this man I count on for
my deeper self, is dead. I sit on a Liverpool
Corporation bus, jolting its dull green way towards
the docks, towards my in-between-things job
with iron ships, hugging a neurotic degree and this,
today's bleak news, past black warehouses, cranes,
listening to elegies inside my head: across
a dozen counties a single violin's exquisite grief.

MATT SIMPSON

The Lark Ascending

Nigel Kennedy is in the kitchen,
where all best talk happens,
trying to tell me something,

I think he wants to bring me
late spring at Llanmadoc,
on my back, in clover, reading

invisible ink on a blue page,
at my ear the tick, tick
of an ant's path through grass,

no, he wants to tell me of the murder
of larks, not an exaltation,
three thousand slaughtered daily,

mostly sent to France,
no, no, elongated arpeggio,
listen, can't you!

something wants to be said
then said and said again,
something I can't catch,

116

can't see at all,
till the song comes clear,
till the whole thing flickers,

tumbles, spirals, stroboscopic,
drops like a stone,
falls as news, the edge of everything,

that rap on the door,
the shout from upstairs,
my thoughts that will not settle

long enough to let the full strings
back him up. The milkman on the step
has Neil Young on his radio

and something in that soaring
Heart of Gold lets Nigel Kennedy
smile at me

over the hum of milkfloat,
the whirr and weight of memory,
his tricky, shimmering flight towards the new.

MAURA DOOLEY

To R. W. Vaughan Williams

Maker of square shaped music, hewer of sound
That has the walking quickened of me on the hills.
The taker of the very sea surge that fills
Granite of Cornish inlets, when the ground
Shakes with the onset. Singer of grove and mound
Also, of Shropshire pastoral quiet, miles
Of roadway have I gone with your marching files
Of ranked lines – Music with Nature's own worthy found.

But in a later day help he would have brought,
Had that but saved me! and I now call to him
To save me from a Fate bitterer than thought
Had guessed; who find Life more than Death's self to be grim.
May he yet save me with high Salvation wrought
Of pity. For here always Hope is obscured and dim.

IVOR GURNEY

Vaughan Williams' Lark Ascending

Request this music at my wake
when everyone's half-canned
on Scotch and almost out
of dissolute affection and it's time
to imagine, to pretend something's riding
upwards out of very soil, something perhaps
(was this what Brooke naively meant?)
embarrassingly English, a longing so
sequestered, as in this, that only love
will know it: that violin way up
over somewhere green like Grantchester
and in a sky so keen and huge
it transforms meadow and slow river
into an illusion of forever; a day
of summer frocks and lovers
reconnoitring each other's mouths
and hearing – bowing it higher, higher –
above the scraping of the spades
this wistful speck of bird.

MATT SIMPSON

To the Man who Wanted a Symphony to Have a Happy Ending

Do not suppose sequence is any clue,
or that serenity following on despair
cancels its pain, for both are true.
Grief's not dethroned by joy, or dark by light
they are man's equal hemispheres of day and night.

Do not suppose succeeding years make plain
a secret code transcribing joy and grief,
interpreting man's journey. This is vain.
Either may perish, either endure through skill;
the spirit is incarnate where it will.

URSULA VAUGHAN WILLIAMS

SERGEI RACHMANINOV (1873–1943)

Coming Late to Rachmaninov

Sergei, I'm forty-three and I've learned to love.
It's middle age, I know.
When we recognize the power we never had
– a post-Romantic flurry of notes and emotion –
is declining. And so I'm driving

past the K-mart, the older part of the new
strip development, Sergei, some holiday
or other, lights screaming in a sky,
pennants at a car lot calling,
and the balding salesmen smile.
'To hell with them,' you once said, 'I don't know how
to write a symphony.'

But I put on my Toyota's warning flashers,
pull to the curb to cry
at the adagio of your Second try.
Among the wrappers and crap from convenience stores,
shards of broken glass like clarinets,
is that theme we scoffed at younger,
da da da DEE da dum,
the styrofoam cups outlasting even the strings,

and nothing changes by your music
except that I am changed.
I walk to the median listening, the traffic passing
while the violins climb your dominant chord
to its beautiful resolution.

You of the passionless melancholy
who thought himself 'a most uninteresting man,'
who wept a little daily, a black well.

RICHARD TERRILL

Rachmaninov

Rachmaninov put his hands terribly to his head
As he found his own First Symphony
Insupportable
And at the end of the first movement
Fled,
Spent the night on a tramcar
Shuttling backwards and forwards.
It was so garish
That his mind broke down.
But it is well known
How he was hypnotised
And returned in triumph
To compose the Second Concerto.

Now I'm Rachmaninov:
Have seen all that dazzle-in-the-dark
And dark-in-the-dazzle,
Have shuttled with wrecked mind between termini,
Recovered in the sternness
Of an obdurate Russian gaze,
Rediscovered winning musical ways.

Shrunk in my furs I menace
With whistling digits
Auditoria rapturously silent
In the spirit of polite adulterous tearooms.

How do you discern my true melody?
Leave the man you were going to be guilty with,
Come to my dressing-room instead.
Though I'm a melancholy exile
I'll more than tell you what I'm like in bed.
We'll play The Isle of the Dead
And while you go on repeating the perfect truth
That my Preludes are underrated
I'll put my hands terribly to my head.

MARTIN SEYMOUR-SMITH

The Isle of the Dead

On the turntable the end
of Rachmaninov's Op 29.

It is the last breath,
the shivering toward silence.

It is the sigh in the cypress
and Charon's exhalation.

What follows is the needle scratch
of oars on gloomy, glassy water

as the craft glides into the bay
below the abandoned temple

and one enters the hearth-cold death
of monophonic silence.

TONY ROBERTS

GUSTAV HOLST (1874–1934)

One of the Planets

Catching the train that day, there opposite
Was Imogen Holst, by chance, recognised
Quite how I don't know. Laid out between us
Sheets of music paper, all the lines and notes
Under her quick bright eye and poised pen
Held almost like a baton.
I could just make out, on the top margin, the name
Gustav – upside down. What she was up to
I was ignorant of, dear devoted daughter
Making her stabbing, almost nervous marks.
But as we approached London
After those hours of fixed concentration,
She looked up, caught my gaze, and a great smile
Irradiated her small neat serious face;
And in my inner ear there soared that tune
Pulsing through Jupiter, the bringer of joy.

ANTHONY THWAITE

Holst

Marching into prayers at primary school
they used to play a 78 of *Mars*.
There began my love of music
and of astronomy. The perfect fool
had found his round peg's round hole:
to sing squarely of the stars
to a generation who would lose its
sight and hearing before it had grown old.

JOHN GREENING

ARNOLD SCHOENBERG (1874–1951)

Shapcott's Variation on Schoenberg's Orchestration of Bach's Prelude and Fugue in E flat major, 'St Anne'

Where does it come from this passion
for layers? I could eat the lexicon,
breathe whole fugues in German and Latin,
rub notes on my skin to make the pores sing.

I love it, like this, when I lose touch
with whose the voice is, whose the fingers
on the bow, the pen, whose mouth
the noise belongs to in the end.

Numbers make me tremble in spring.
I want to counterpoint them until I careen
off the edge of the world disputing
with God himself about the number seven.

JO SHAPCOTT

MAURICE RAVEL (1875–1937)

On Playing Ravel's Concerto for the Left Hand

Someone in the Green Room will always ask
Aren't you tempted to use both hands
and halve the difficulty – either way

the music's the same, isn't it? No.
It's not. Music can never be 'the same.'
What do they know about exhilaration,

about the essence of gesture? So I smile
and ask in return *And an arabesque …*
would it be as graceful on two legs?

GREGORY WARREN WILSON

Ravel at Swim

The inability to communicate speech, writing or music when the peripheral
nervous system is largely undamaged is called an aphasia.
                              John O'Shea, *Maurice Ravel: Aspects of Musical Perception*

Something dark has stolen the sea from me.
Always a seal in water, I found its
melodies and swam open harmony
through them. Now I flail. Nothing I do fits

the rhythms around me. *Swiss Watchmaker*
they called me for the design of my work.
Mere lover of wind-up toys, a baker
of sweets, as though elegance were a quirk.

Now the hand that holds forks by their tines floats
like driftwood on the sea of music spread
before me. It will not copy the notes
I hear like a gull's bent tones in my head.

It will not play what I see on paper
and know I wrote two years ago to be
performed one-handed. That was a caper!
I loved having such limits placed on me.

It will not sign my name. It tries to light
a match with the tip of a cigarette.
What is left? It took me eight days to write
a fifty-six word letter I have yet

to end, consoling a friend whose mother
just died. I do not want to be seen now
by anyone who knew me at another
time. Pure artifice, they said, missing how

my need for form affirmed the passions of
my heart. They must not see me with the link
from brain to limb severed and all I love
lost. Sheer formlessness surrounds me. I think

but cannot share my thoughts. I remember
every flower's fragrance, the taste of lamb
roasted for hours over charcoal embers
at summer bazaars, lips on mine, but am

powerless to express myself. Let me
be alone. Let me have the grace of pure
music in my head, where I hear and see
perfectly. That silence I can endure.

FLOYD SKLOOT

OTTORINO RESPIGHI (1879–1936)

The Pines of Rome

(for Katherine & Royston)

As ghosts of old legionaries, or the upright
farmers of that unbelievable republic,
the pines entail their roots among the rubble
    of baroque and modern Rome.

Out by the catacombs they essay a contradiction,
clattering their chariot-blade branches to deny
the Christian peace, the tourist's easy frisson,
    a long transfiguration.

Look away from Agnes and the bird-blind martyrs,
the sheep of God's amnesia, the holy city
never built, to the last flag of paganism
    flying in mosaic.

Then say the pines, though we are Papal like the chill
water of the aqueducts, refreshment from a state
divinity, we know that when they tombed the martyrs
    they ambushed them with joy.

Rome is all in bad taste and we are no exception
is their motto. Small wonder that Respighi, 'the last Roman',
adds recorded nightingales to his score *The Pines*
    of the Janiculum.

And the scent of pines as we dine at night
among the tethered goats and the Egyptian waiters
is a promise that everything stays forever foreign
    which settles down in Rome.

Therefore I nominate a Roman pine to
stand above my slab, and order a mosaic
of something small and scaly to represent
    my soul on its last journey.

PETER PORTER

BÉLA BARTÓK (1881–1945)

On Hearing Bartók's Concerto for Orchestra

Instinct with the division of labour peals
The sonorous and manufactured brass:
The lonely instrument and player caught
    And transcended by the mass.

At such art in our time one cannot help
But think with love and terror of the double
Man, and the puzzling dumb notation under
    Floors of the future's rubble.

ROY FULLER

The King of Swords

Will you follow me light, into the dark?
Will you clothe the walls
in your sun-steeped pelt
oh creature of gold, will you follow?

Secure the door, remove your shoes
ignore the dissonant score
that etches your bones
and the blood-specked notes in the clouds.

I could master time for you;
preserve your bloom in a jar.
I could leech the day from you
as easy as turning a key.
See, my castle weeps for you!
Will you follow me love, will you follow?

HELEN IVORY

Bartók

It wasn't a style as such, the way they wore
their hats and waistcoats, laboured through the mud
or gathered at the inn. Hard to make a score
of what they sang, the odd shriek and thud,
that nasal whine, the raw polyphony
of their existence. You had to record it all
on the latest equipment, pay them good money
for performing, listen to them call
the devil into the heart of the authentic,
his melancholy to the tongue's rough edge.
It can't have been easy to shift their strangely frantic
strings into the concert hall. It was knowledge
but not as we knew it, nor was it desired.
It screeched and snapped like bullets freshly fired.

Music was war. It was the sound of guns
wheeled into position and the cry of men
in ditches. Music was prophetic. Once
it lodged in the ear the worst would surely happen.
Those women were the wind howling. Rain
was rapid rifles. Concert halls were wrecked,
the century blown wide open. The troop train
would never arrive, and nothing would connect.
The barbarians were always at the gate,
but they were us and now we had burst in
to what we had forgotten. We were late:
our villages were bodies and burned skin.
A voice emerged. It was the voice we shared.
Now we could listen. Now we were prepared.

GEORGE SZIRTES

IGOR STRAVINSKY (1882–1971)

Petrushka (Stravinsky)

Till now, to others: when at last it happens
it hurts less finally than the dolls believe:
the hand that held the puppets falls and opens;
the puppets twist, and rise, and are alive.
But now they can no longer move together –
though (look) the strings are tangled. The freed limb
searches for muscles to replace its tether;
the muscles have no music ruling them.
But up, slack-sinewed; and a kind of bow
(no longer to a fellow) to the mirror;
then, out of habit, part of the old dance.
Look once around no-longer-home. And now
learn that your world had edges; and, with terror,
stare out across the waiting audience.

TERENCE TILLER

Concert-Interpretation

(Le Sacre du Printemps)

The audience pricks an intellectual Ear …
Stravinsky … Quite the Concert of the Year!

Forgetting now that none-so-distant date
When they (or folk facsimilar in state
Of mind) first heard with hisses – hoots – guffaws –
This abstract Symphony (they booed because
Stravinsky jumped their Wagner palisade
With modes that seemed cacophonous and queer),
Forgetting now the hullabaloo they made,
The Audience pricks an intellectual ear.

Bassoons begin ... Sonority envelops
Our auditory innocence; and brings
To Me, I must admit, some drift of things
Omnific, seminal, and adolescent.
Polyphony through dissonance develops
A serpent-conscious Eden, crude but pleasant;
While vibro-atmospheric copulations
With mezzo-forte mysteries of noise
Prelude Stravinsky's statement of the joys
That unify the monkeydom of nations.

This matter is most indelicate indeed!
Yet one perceives no symptom of stampede.
The Stalls remain unruffled: craniums gleam:
Swept by a storm of pizzicato chords,
Elaborate ladies re-assure their lords
With lifting brows that signify 'Supreme!'
While orchestrated gallantry of goats
Impugns the astigmatic programme-notes.

In the Grand Circle one observes no sign
Of riot: peace prevails along the line.
And in the Gallery, cargoed to capacity,
No tremor bodes eruptions and alarms.
They are listening to this not-quite-new audacity
As though it were by someone dead, – like Brahms.

But savagery pervades Me; I am frantic
With corybantic rupturing of laws.
Come, dance, and seize this clamorous chance to function
Creatively, – abandoning compunction
In anti-social rhapsodic applause!
Lynch the conductor! Jugulate the drums!
Butcher the brass! Exsanguinate the strings!
Throttle the flutes! ... Stravinsky's April comes
With pitiless pomp and pain of sacred springs ...
Incendiarize the Hall with resinous fires
Of sacrificial fiddles scorched and snapping! ...

Meanwhile the music blazes and expires;
And the delighted Audience is clapping.

SIEGFRIED SASSOON

Venice April 1971

Three black gondolas
cut the sparkle of the lagoon.

In the first, the Greek archimandrite
stands, a young black-bearded man
in gold cope, black hood, black shoulder veil blown back
in the sunny breeze. In front of him
his even younger acolyte holds high
the glittering processional cross. His long black robe
glitters with delicious silver flowers
against the blue of the sky.

In the second gondola Stravinsky goes.
The black fringe trails the lapping water,
the heavy coffin dips the golden lions on the sides,
the gondoliers are ankle-deep in roses,
the coffin sways crowned with roses,
the gondoliers' white blouses and black sashes
startle their brown arms, the shining oars,
the pink and crimson flowers.

And the third gondola
is like a shadow
where the widow goes.

And there at the edge of the picture
where the crowds cross themselves
and weep a little in the Italian way,
an old poet with white hair
and hooded, piercing eyes
leans on his stick
and without expression
watches the boats move out
from his shore.

EDWIN MORGAN

PERCY GRAINGER (1882–1961)

Musicians Rehearsing al fresco

They hold down their music with plastic clothes-pegs
(the light, April wind blustering *adagio assai*
over the paddock where newly-born lambs are grazing);
First Violin flicks blossom from his Cremona fiddle

with birthday-cake fingers, while Fräulein D'Amore
picks out *In an English Country Garden, a tempo giusto*,
on her viola. Madame Svoboda curses the barbed wire
that threatens her cellocase, and measures the horsehair

of her second-best bow against some bayard strands
caught on the fence-snaggings. From the milking sheds
rise the clatter of harpsichords and a flute trilling
and falling, the first flutter of conversations

between brass and woodwind. The Violins, grown impatient,
exchange glances, rapping music stands. The Estate trees
flurry, and heave to attention. The bows drop in fury.
They savage the notes off the stave, like mad dogs.

JOHN GOHORRY

ARNOLD BAX (1883–1953)

A Girl's Music

Among the piano's fire-lit keys
Intoxicate her fingers creep.
Ah cease! they make one near to weep,
These unskilled poignant melodies.

What vicious-hearted djinn has sent
Such tortured beauty to this child,
Making her drunken with these wild
Sad dronings of the Orient?

Some half-thing sure she must recall
Of furious splendour, gorgeous lust,
Claiming her through the wind and dust
Of crumbling ages' lapse and fall.

The spell still sways her inwardly,
The dream burns in her languid eyes,
While almost angrily she tries
To re-invoke her tragedy

And the gorged drowsy fiend who gloats
On her half-naked loveliness
That in the dance nigh fainting floats
Through the hot scents, whilst all the place

Vibrates with rhythmic hammerings,
With thunderous noise of pear-shaped drums,
And some hunched rocking goblin thrums
Outlandishly on golden strings.

I think they bade her dance and die
In one night's fume and din and shame,
For in this music throbs the same
Fierce weariness and ecstasy.

DERMOT O'BYRNE (a.k.a. Arnold Bax)

ANTON WEBERN (1883–1945)

For the Death of Anton Webern Particularly

Sunday gardening, hoeing, trying to think of nothing but
hoeing – so that this at least can be an exercise in the true sense –
nevertheless I can think of little but the death of Anton Webern.
I just happened to read it. It just happened to be Webern.
One has ferreted out and written up at length how the Weberns
went out to dine some night with their daughter and their
(unbeknown to them) blackmarketeer of a son-in-law, shortly
after the American occupation. The G.I. agent provocateur went out
to block any escape. Just at that moment, in the black back yard,
the fragile Webern, out to puff a gift cigar, collided
with the decoy who shot him by mistake. Back home, not knowing
whom he'd killed, but withered by it, this kind man died of drink.

Sunday gardening, hoeing, I turn over the worms in their beds
and am shadowed by the blackbirds. And I have to ask again from what
body-stitching those worms are sundered and picked out writhing to die,
and from what soul-harrowing that Rome of blackbirds flutters down
to drill and gut the worms with javelin beaks, and in the fold of what
wedding of body and desire in Jerusalem I am conceived and born
to offer this show. I need to ask on what Sunday God first churned
his cauldron world in such a manner that we all deal death,
not knowing that we deal it, scarcely caring, yet dying of it too
from afar – in what stew God first mixed meat of worm,
feather and beak of bird and hand of man and what bubbles
send up each in turn to do the other in. And how, at last, the notes
composed by fragile Webern survive the boil and music in the bubbles.

NATHANIEL TARN

After Webern

How to make sense of the unnerving
intervals played on the strings? And what if
the occluded cries rising from the debris
of our enmity
                mix with the atonal world
I've ventured into? I've muted

the bows on the hi-fi, and in a little while
I'll have hammered myself

a sonnet-gone-awry that might
speak to our times. – Dear Anton, forgive me
for wrestling your broken, melodic
line to the ground this way,
                    but the skies, the skies
are pierced with wrath, as they would be
for you, stepping outside for air, the slug
spinning you to the dust.

January 18, 2009

GABRIEL LEVIN

The Music Cleaner

in memory of George Jack

The cleaner pechs at night
Up steep, worn treads of arpeggios,

Polishing, brushing between octaves
With rasping bristles, now and then

Camel hairs for finicky work,
So the song's dust-free again, catches you out.

Relishing the life of Anton Webern
Who stepped outside one night into the curfew,

Lit up a cigarette, and was shot dead,
Songs taken to the cleaners have big souls

Roomy enough for cigarette and gunshot.
Plainchant, birds in spinifex, ululations,

Every song that is must have a cleaner,
To let it know how God is in the details

Public as the sky right now above you,
Private as your own ears, listening.

ROBERT CRAWFORD

ALBAN BERG (1885–1935)

Alban Berg's Violin Concerto

Dem Andenken eines Engels

I don't know what she said –
that nineteen year angel who fell
into the prefigurement of his own death:

   a world before and after the struggle

'Perhaps I can live
one ... two months more?'

It is enough.

She died:
her paralysis
became a vision of dancing
towards the irresistible catastrophe
and resolution – the arch of a violin
holding a Bach Chorale.

He too died:
in great pain, it is said,
but from his bed his arms spread
in winged delirium:
'An up-beat! An up-beat!'

Es ist genug.

His death-mask is quiet.

PETER JONES

GEORGE BUTTERWORTH (1885–1916)

Rhapsody

In memory of George Butterworth

George Butterworth whose name meant nothing to me
those five years I biked up and down my school drive
under chestnuts bare or flaunting their cream candelabras
past the lodge where he wrote *The Banks of Green Willow*.

The same George Butterworth who today I encounter
dancing on You Tube a folk medley in Burford in 1913
sporting white flannels, white handkerchief, knee-bells
and drooping moustache before these things turned quaint.

George Butterworth who three years later was shot dead
not ducking low enough in his trench and whose melodies
now will never stop pouring out over the wire and mud
where he lay down in his dark uniform his darkened head.

ANDREW MOTION

BOHUSLAV MARTINŮ (1890–1959)

Frances Dancing with Martinů

Light shines through your eyes
and you would dance as well as play.
The score before you holds you
but your feet won't stay.
And this is Martinů and you,
and we, the audience are in it too.

Five lines, and five, and five again
the page hung with ellipses
some in solitary, hollow state
command your bow to draw
its length across the string
and others, black, trip hand in hand,
take you up ladder-lines
and off the top
or tumble, space through space
until a cadence catches them.

Curved lines sweep over
melismatic flow;
staccato dots break in.
Where blocks and squiggles
let you snatch a breath
the bow flicks up and off,
the strings are singing still.

You show us how
he put the signs in line
to tell you what he felt.
You take the page of symbols,
put the music back
and we are privileged to join
the dance with Martinů and you.

HELEN ASHLEY

IVOR GURNEY (1890–1937)

Masterpiece

Out from the dim mind like dark fire rises thought,
And one must be quick on it … or scratch sketches, a few …

And later, three weeks later, in fashion sedater,
See, the night worker writing his square work out,
Set to the labour, muscle strained, his light hidden under.
Half-past two? Time for tea … Half-past, half-past two …
And then by degrees of half hours see how it shows:
The pages fill with black notes, the paper-bill goes
Up and up, till the musician is left staring
At a String Quartett nobody in the world will do …
And what Schumann would say there's no one to be caring.

Now, had it been a joke or some wordy, windy poem
About Destiny or Fatal-Way or Weltmuth or Sarsparilla,
London would have hugged to it like a glad gorilla …
Happy to know its deepest heart told out so,
Deepest conviction, or maxim driven so home
(To the next door neighbour). But since the new making is still a
Mere Quartett for Strings after the Beethoven way,
With no aspiration to say more than ever was said
By Beethoven; expecting such treatment and casual pay;
The musician is left to turn over Shakespeare and to find
Favourite passages when the dim East shows blind.
Get rid of his drink how he may, blamed for such drinking;
Leave his MS there, wondering what neighbours may be thinking
Of people who work a week through without end
And neither Lyons, Lipton or the London String Quartett
To care much what high glory from the light glory came to command;
Or – see … how the two tunes into one English picture came linking.

IVOR GURNEY

Gurney: At the Front

Was it a mine? To me Aladdin's cave
       More like,
Or really like a mine shaft candle lit,
       So in we crawled

And naturally, the men were Welsh, pit men. I felt
       So much
At home, for instantly, it seems, rather than speak
       We fell to song

And it was music to my soul, the Celt
       In me,
And with them I felt so much less the freak
       I had for long …

And I was glad to wear a uniform
       That held
Me inextricably bound up with others.
       But did I care

For war or England's glory? No, the storm
       I felt
Was something different. And still it bothers
       Me as I stare

So vacantly at these asylum walls
       So smooth
And ask whatever happened to the prop
       That held me up

With them (crouched down like animals in stalls
       Of straw)
And felt the good fatigue that let me drop
       Like wine into a cup …

I never felt like that again,
       That first
Night I experienced the tingling thrill
       With men unharmed

Who triumphed over bitter wind and rain
       And hail
Of bullets and bombs' thunder which their still
       Strong voices calmed …

Yes, I remember all the thrill it gave
      Me there
As now I live a freak show in the pit
      In which life stalled.

N. S. THOMPSON

To a Christian Concerning Ivor Gurney

You will have much to explain to your God on the final day,
And he, also, will have much to explain to you –
Why (say) the mind of Gurney, whose preludes I am listening to,
Should, through so many years, have to waste away
Into inconsequence – composer, poet who dreamed that our land
Would greet in him an heir of Jonson and Dowland;
But its mind was elsewhere, and so was that of your Lord,
Assigning this soldier his physical composition –
That blood, those chromosomes that drew him to the absurd
Disordering of notes, to the garrulity of the word,
Instead of the forms that already his youthful passion
Had prepared for the ordering of both self and nation.

CHARLES TOMLINSON

SERGEI PROKOFIEV (1891–1953)

From *Nuncle Music*

Sergei Prokofiev is dead
hung in the air
like an impossibility.

Prokofiev, one of my deaf spots.
So, is the weather here always like this?

No one should dare to die
on the same day as Stalin,
but Sergei beat the Wolf to it
by fifty minutes.

I wasn't there to wave them off
into versts of Elysian field
where thin ghosts flock and jostle
to hear the Five-Year Plans,
the forevers and foralways,
of our club-footed orator Wolf.

No wreaths for Sergei,
the Wolf had snaffled the lot,
while soul upon soul choked to death
in the crush for peeks at the corpse.

I might risk now a musical portrait
of the Kremlin Mountaineer,
not my old thunder, sonic diarrhoea,
writhings and rollings, overwritten
to stifle terror and drawn out thought,

but instead I punch out one last time
D S C H.

Let the Wolf howl.
After him, mere mortals.

GARETH REEVES

PETER WARLOCK (Philip Heseltine)
(1894–1930)

Elegy for Philip Heseltine

Wildheart is dead. Plumage of heavenly hue,
  Bright eye, bold wing, ardour and grief and rage,
Some snatches of sweet song – all, all too few! –
  Then the dead feathers dulling in the cage.
Wildheart is dead. The story's nothing new.

The story's nothing new. Wildheart is dead.
  And now the all-too-intolerably wise
May stroke the chin and sigh and wag the head.
  To the devil with them and their pious lies!
Lord, they mean well. But see the wing half spread.

Wildheart is dead and the vehement wings at rest
  Battered so hard against the wire and wood.
Wildheart is still. He has whistled his brave best.
  Wildheart, dear Wildheart, lie now where you should
Gathered, heart's brother, to your poet's breast!

ROBERT NICHOLS

FRANCIS POULENC (1899–1963)

Playing Cards with Poulenc

'Manic-depressive' would be the old term; up one
minute, down the next – the source of the tussle
in his *Gloria*, as it veers from riotous to reverential.

Or was it inspired as he claimed by a combination
of Gozzoli's frescoes of angels, tongues sticking out,
and the Benedictine monks he watched playing football?

A pointer to his mood-swings: when out for a stroll
he'd turn his hat-brim up or down to inform passers-by
whether he wanted to chat or be left alone. Some saw this

as attention-seeking: what's more important – the way
you look at the world, or the way the world looks at you?
Perhaps part of a wider pattern: as Prokofiev's partner

at the bridge table did his bids betray his frame of mind;
hearts and diamonds for joy, black suits for depression?
When after a separation of twenty years Prokofiev died,

Poulenc began an oboe sonata in memory of the friend
who had once urged him to enter a bridge contest,
the prize dwarfing anything he was likely to earn

from musical composition. A further decade gone
prior to its completion, its première was delayed
until after his own death – the last card Fate dealt him.

STEWART CONN

AARON COPLAND (1900–90)

Appalachian Spring

We don't know where we are really, or when,
only that the instruments occur
like something not yet said. A year
newly broken from the swift red flesh

of winter, a barn newly built
on rocky confidence, allow
a brief planned carelessness
an octave deeper into the earth.

Prayer is almost comical in this abundance,
fate a minor key that's left unplayed.
This reminder courses through the woodwinds,
turns in open fields. Faith says

landscape is there. Faith and works
return *a tempo* in the greening hills,
the unmemorized lines of animals.
Pieces of sunlight cut from a cloth is sky.

It's a simple gift to know what can be taken from us.
The last time through, the piano beats time,
the cellos pray again, the preacher simply ignored,
the new Americans quiet in their house of myth.

Shakers have no descendants and therefore must have faith
in cycles of work, day and death.
No night closes over their eyes
cello and obbligato haven't foreshadowed.

RICHARD TERRILL

GERALD FINZI (1901–56)

Finzi's Orchard

There is special power in an adoptive landscape,
Unsmudged by ties of birth or ancestry,
Unburnished by false childhood memory.

Hampshire downland: Church Farm, Ashmansworth.
'This,' he said, 'is what I have always longed for.'
Not meaning, I think, anything as easy

As an edenic ideal, but rather the place
To do what he did best: to cultivate
Rare apple trees, collect rare poets, write

An English music – more than English because
His outsider's eye and ear have given it
Such frail disenchantment, such haunted repose.

Shakespeare, Milton, Traherne, Wordsworth, Hardy:
Their words are kerned, finding new edges,
New spaces between them, and new purity

Of diction. There is fresh wind in the trees;
A russet windfall nestles in the grass;
The russet clarinet rests on its bed of strings.

NEIL POWELL

MICHAEL TIPPETT (1905–98)

Listening to Tippett Twice: A Child of Our Time (1944)

South Kensington now
I'm early at the table
wait patiently with a beer
then rise with a kiss to greet her

and my day's been real
in the absence of dreams
so ordinary real
to include the buying of bread

then making a few calls
coffee and a newspaper's
rancour and grief
and time always fixing times –

now a wash of notes
tentatively rising
from the well of the hall
though it's hard to give them

the attention they need
with these nervous coughs
firing like gunshots
but as muted trumpets

stir the choir to its feet
I'm gone a thousand miles
I've gone twenty years
into the sunlight

of a baked-brown hillside
near Assisi I remember
as a sloping orchard
close to the end of summer

at the mouth of a tent
I gaze at sweltering heat
alone but thinking of her
across the Alps

beyond the Channel
my earphones growling
with these same notes –
I've no money for my bread

I have no gift for my love
the tenor's plight rolling
on a spool of tape
running steadily down

like a little clock of longing
though within a week
I'll have re-crossed Europe
fallen into her arms

set foot on the path
to where this tenor's lament
asks the same redemption
from two hundred voices

weepingly as one
these voices concluding
at last with silence
the pause of reluctance

as we pick up the threads
of the evening we realise
what our hands are for
moving to defer words

unless it is in this way
to try to repeat the gift
of the dreamwork
of the singers against

the dreamwork of the past
to fling it forward
against rancour and grief
against the coming need

MARTYN CRUCEFIX

To an English Composer

Landscapes flourish best
indoors. Here's one
you turned into music, green
in lush dissonance with green,
forty years ago. It glows

again. I carry it among
un-English rocks and rain
thinking – real English fields
would also lie untouched
by this ghost they fled. It flows

through fields and memories
of fields that gave and then forgot
and now rest weightless,
real ghosts that fail to touch
this burgeoning pastoral
with their mundane repose.

ROBIN FULTON MACPHERSON

DMITRY SHOSTAKOVICH (1906–75)

Prelude

So, who do you suppose paid for your talent?
Not you, boy; not your parents.

Who trained you? fed you with extra rations?
You'd have died as a student

when the tuberculosis swelled your neck,
without that post-operative stay

in the expensive State Sanatorium,
the convalescence by the Black Sea –

from which came …? only
'a trio for first love'!

Better watch your step, boy!
We could still cut your throat.

Who spirited you out of Leningrad
in spite of the insult of that opera?

Don't you think we have the right
to expect some gratitude,

some music to express the soul of your people
instead of this selfish 'self-expression'?

Elitism's a dead-end road –
look at the grim stones left

by those who've tried to travel along it!
You should realise, boy,

that you owe us, that we've got you in an armlock,
that you'll compose what we want, or nothing.

JOANNA BOULTER

A Postscript to Shostakovich's Reply

I hear the music of the dead from a great distance,
not the voices of the known but of the unknown
who died under snow, or of an infamous hunger.

Speechless, they speak now in your music –
cries torn on the wind, tears blown into splinters.
Out of the grey sky I see their arms, thin as rain.

Such music comes from a long suffering
and how can we know pain who have not felt
the torturer's iron, or weep if we've not seen
the bones of children swept into the street?

Then let it rain all winter on this land
for nothing now can drown the voices of the dead
who cry within the comfort of my room
or in shocked eyes defy the hollowness of stars.

EDWARD STOREY

1943

(Shostakovich: Symphony No. 8 in C Minor)

Earth, and then, a handful of glass, sharp,
the silver thread of firstmorninglight.
Early hours. In the early hours,
when they'll come, or when they might come,
or when they do. In the shadows, in the half-light,
in the small hours, first ice, fear and its children,
the wet birch leaves slapping the window.
The mind turns against day. Against day.
The land, dark under rain, snow, heavy skies,
the land itself then closes like a door.

MAURA DOOLEY

Ode to Dmitri Shostakovich

I

To what far room of never-to-return
The raw brass singles out and calls us –
A tale too often told, one old already
Long before the pen of Mandelstam
Entangled itself in the Georgian's moustaches.
Those feelers found him out, and you survived
To play the fool and to applaud the play
That you must act in. Notes told less than words
And now tell more, each vast adagio dense
With the private meaning of its public sorrow.

II

You stole the Fate Motif from Wagner's *Ring*
(Great artists steal and minor merely borrow) –
Fate had declared itself as daily fact:
This day might be the allotted span. Tomorrow …?
Stalin was dead. But not his heirs, and not
The memory imprinted in the nerves, the heart.
Light-eared, light-fingered, you had earned your share
Of that absurd prestissimo from *William Tell*,
To accompany an endlessly running man
In one of the silent comedies of nightmare.

III

Inscribing score on score with your motto theme –
Mnemonic of survival, notes for a name –
'I am still here,' you signal, yet once more,
And now that you no longer are, the same
Chime recurring takes on the whole of time
Out of a permanence few of us can have.
In the photograph you pass smiling to the grave.

CHARLES TOMLINSON

Sausage

(fantasia on Valentin Berlinsky's anecdote about the Eighth Quartet)

It was an honour to be asked to play,
while they were still at the conservatoire.
So they worked on it for days, weeks,
despite their almost constant hunger.
Since he'd quoted freely from his work,
they decided he meant it as an epitaph
to a life's staggering achievements.

His flat was in surprising disarray
but, on the upright piano, sausage,
bread and vodka had been arranged.
Their tempo was a little fast,
but they'd been told that, in general,
this suited the state of his nerves –
and they avoided looking at the food.

At the end they paused, stunned.
He stood a moment without speaking –
then left the room. They waited,
throats dry; he didn't return.
Imagine the humiliation. How they felt
that they had failed him! How hungrily
each packed his instrument and left.

But the next day he sent apologies;
he'd been overcome by the performance.
They should play the piece that way.
They gathered round their cold hearth,
ablaze with the news of his approval.
They joked about burning his note
for warmth, and laughed at their irreverence.

Then, inevitably, the four reminisced.
One remembered the glint of glasses;
another returned to those pianissimo chords.
But the cellist blushed before admitting
how slow he'd been to realise: it wasn't
the sausage in that cramped apartment
that provided the piquancy, but the score.

TONY ROBERTS

OLIVIER MESSIAEN (1908–92)

Messiaen's Piano

Messiaen's piano
throws notes like handfuls of stones
to clatter
against a glass-
house God:
           birds'
arrhythmic hearts,
they're precipitated into the bluster
and terror of spring.

The beautiful world hardly responds
yet these go on – chorus, soloist. *Make a joyful noise*
unto the Lord.

Are you glass –
your absence a mirror?
                      Well, I lob stones.
Far off,
as from a distant copse,
hear what bodies do:
suspension,
interruption.
That long, perfect fall.

FIONA SAMPSON

Messiaen

for Christel and Alexander Baillie

Conceived and written in the course of my captivity, the Quartet for the End
of Time *was performed for the first time in Stalag-A on January 15, 1941 …*

Olivier Messiaen

1

Slowly, as the theme
Becomes your face,
Its agonies of grace
Appal, yet seem
At rest, declare
All pain resolved
To liberty and held
On safe, immaculate air.

2

The pizzicato of a quick
Grief plucks at its bars –
Your dreams release each prisoner's
Pride from his panic.

3

The world prepares its instruments. Whoever cries
Keeps time with Time and learns to temporise.

4

After the last held note
Returns us to ourselves, we cling
To your gift, the sustaining
Promise of silence,
And we live in hope
As you did, as your innocence
Survived the cut-throat
Darkness of Europe.

JOHN MOLE

SAMUEL BARBER (1910–81)

A Note on Barber's Adagio

for Dónal Gordon

… Back in autumn 1963
Samuel Barber was alone and driving through
November rain in Iowa or Kansas.
When he turned on his radio he heard
Them playing his *Adagio for Strings*.
Sick to death of his most famous composition,
He turned the dial through the static
Until once again, and clearly –
The *Adagio for Strings*. When a third station, too,
And then a fourth, were playing it, he thought
He must be going mad. He turned off the radio
And stopped the car and got out by a fence
Staring at the endless open space in front of him
Where someone on a tractor plowed
On slowly in the rain …

The president had been assassinated
Earlier that day, but Barber didn't know it yet.
He only knew that every station in America was playing
His *Adagio for Strings*.
He only knew he didn't know
Why he should be responsible for such an ecstasy of grief.

JOHN MATTHIAS

American Music

Samuel Barber asked for croutons to be scattered at his funeral.
From the cortège, as the fresh soil steamed, adagio,
Feldman, Carter, Crumb and all the products of Boulanger
approached to salute and pepper him with their hard pieces.

JOHN GREENING

JOHN CAGE (1912–92)

The Old Man comes out with an Opinion

This long orchestral piece records a day
the composer spent one summer meditating
in Dibnah's yard on the sounds of dereliction,
or possibly the dereliction of sound:

the settlement of rust, the flake and drift
toward the earth of forged and hammered things,
the creak of shiny flanges in the wind,
and the occasional crash of martial metal
as boys dribbled a biscuit box along
between the ornamental tetanus hedges
of Fred's Versailles, parterres of ferrous oxide.

Sometimes I wish that Fred's new crush-compactor
had crumpled the composer (*violin solo*)
and his jalopy (*piano, timpani*)
in one bright ingot, multicoloured foil
(*cymbals*), and hoyed the lot in the canal

(a genuine *splash!*, an *hommage to John Cage*).

ALISTAIR ELLIOT

Cage

The composer, locked in a soundproof room in Harvard
Heard his heartbeat and the sound of Niagara Falls
Produced by the operation of his nervous system,
From which he derived a theory, no doubt.

Me, I heard a throaty click at the end of 'wedlock'.
And Niagara on the long-distance line.
I knew a couple once, went up there on their honeymoon.
After a week, they said, you don't even hear it.

MICHAEL DONAGHY

BENJAMIN BRITTEN (1913–76)

Lament for Ben

(to Schubert's Trio *Opus 42)*

Is life, this life, his life
  now lost, was that a dream,
And death, a dream too?
  Whose sleep, whose dream
  Are we who live?
This death, his death
makes all of us die too.
  His life was ours;
  His death is ours;
We grieve, for whom?
We grieve for ourselves.

May Bach and Purcell
Bend down to this bier
But let music sing
to sing their song
Their song, their song
Though poetry's dumb.

In this waste, this grief
these notes alone lend us
    yield us
    give us
    some relief
      though brief
      though brief

RONALD DUNCAN

The Aldeburgh Band

Somehow a mouth-organist
has got into the flue
of the gas stove in the Baptist Chapel.

Every minute or two
she draws a plaintive chord
that dies as the north-easterly
roars in the stack
and the blue flames leap.

But it's in the gazebo
painted star-white,
all the benches wet with mist and fret,
that I recognise what's happened:

when the timpanist plays hide-and-seek
and beats his tiresome tom-tom
in whichever cubicle I'm not,

I soon see or, rather, hear
the whole ragged band
is billeted piecemeal
around Aldeburgh.

So, for instance, the fat man
with the alpenhorn
has found his way into the massive
stone head of the sea-god –
Aegir, president of the flint-grey waves
– and he keeps bellowing in my ear
every time I pass him.

There's a pretty lutanist
behind that lattice window
on Crabbe Path;
whenever she leans out,
she runs her light fingers
along the modillion.

And the contralto with the treacly voice:
there's no escaping her!
She's always under sail, beating
up and down the windy High Street,
decked in globs of amber.

But where's the maestro
– some say magician?
Is he locked in the foundation
or under the long-eared eaves, still
tuning in?
The Aldeburgh Band:
did he have a hand in this?
Those who tell don't know.
Those who know don't tell.

Darkness comes in to land and I walk
along the beach
past the very last silent fisherman
with his lantern
and ghostly-green umbrella.
Crunchcrunch under my feet. Crunchcrunch.

Down to the water's edge
and still the music's everywhere:
all the strings night-bathing
and phosphorescent,
playing glissando;

the stray with the cor anglais,
lonely as a whimbrel
over dark water;

and far away,
far under the glagolitic ocean,
the now-legendary player
of the tubular bells.

KEVIN CROSSLEY-HOLLAND

Borodins and Vodka

For Dmitri Shebalin

A resident quartet.
A form of words, and yet
Through catastrophic days
This bleak eroded coast
Provides, as it has done
Before, safe anchorage.
Resident: at worst
Administrative fiction;
At best, true habitation,
Huge vodkas in the Keys.

There's something in the air
Of Suffolk-Russian kinship:
How many programmes pair
Britten-Shostakovich.
And Ben's interpreters:
Richter, Rostropovich.
A chill from the sea, perhaps;
The windy never-stillness
Impels us to create
Our best, our better-than.

Evenings we'll not forget:
That January storm
Percussed the Maltings roof
(Tchaikovsky 3 beneath);
Fine Easter miniatures
Or Summer Russian masters
With family connections
In eloquent sonatas;
A form of words, and yet
A resident quartet.

NEIL POWELL

Coventry

Even if not sent there, some would go
just to visit a byword for banishment, or
nod and smile at Tudor cottages
verifying their age among highways
athrottle with the local Jaguar –
nine centuries ago the route of (do
they know for certain?) Godiva's midday ride
through narrow, cobbled streets. Still there, and nude,
a statue on a civic pedestal,
she serves as patron for the recent mall.

St. Michael's ruin has no plans to recover
from the blitzkrieg fires of 1940
visibly content with its roof of sky,
a brownstone sheepfold with fence of ogives,
tracery drained of blood-red or river-
blue glass. A few steps north, in autumn sun,
the adjunct modernist cathedral proves
by inscription that Britten's sharp baton
rode lightly above the *War Requiem*
as, borrowing the tenor of Peter Pears,

Wilfred Owen back from the fields of France
grafted his words onto the older hymn
under the eyes of a merciful giant.
The clash of arms turned music of the spheres
to counteract a deadly expedient
how many thousands now cannot denounce.
Black swallows rise and circle as bells chime
the congregants inside at Evensong,
as if war'd been a roughhewn cornerstone
in the edifice of Common Market peace.

Et lux perpetua luceat eis:
Owen, Britten, Pears, all three moved out
of earshot to that other Coventry,
attendants of the blessed lady, prompted
perhaps by music's blinding insights. Is it
because an icon forfeits all privacy
that every bystander at last is tempted,
eye at keyhole or shutter? – this means you,
Peeping Tom, and I, and you, oh,
on fire to see the last thing we will ever see.

ALFRED CORN

162

WITOLD LUTOSŁAWSKI (1913–94)

Playing Lutoslawski in Grasmere Church

Is tragedy suitable at any time?
Can sun or holidays lend a rhyme,
as they did today, calling us from here
to Warsaw in one long drawing of a bow?
Yes, at any time, and better
coming from a player who was born
so the programme says, way after the music.
All so young, and into youthfulness was slipped
this whisper from the camps.
In the heart of the festival and the heat,
the funeral days were back.

DAVID SCOTT

GYÖRGY LIGETI (1923–2006)

Ground Offensive

Now it's Ligeti's turn, his black music
pulled over your face like a stocking in cutthroat
dread, and you make to reach out

and stop its advance but it slams you back
against the wall – this isn't what you wanted,
this is *agitato*, this is micropolyphonic,

as if you knew what that meant, but go on,
the Transylvanian child in you says: I'm your hostage,
let the alpenhorn sound its warning as white

phosphorus streaks the skies, tell me, what
has become of us, boom, boom, boom –
those are electrodes you took for earphones.

GABRIEL LEVIN

HARRISON BIRTWISTLE (b.1934)

After The Minotaur

The steps down to the labyrinth
narrow, steep
light up as each innocent
descends. The ladder lights up
immediately as their descent begins
so of course the ladder was there
all the time, it's there all the time
but it takes the touch
of human flesh, hands on
on the topmost rung to make it
light up. And once lit it stays lit
marking the descent
of the innocents, one by one
and we cannot help but see
the full extent of it
one steep journey made of individual steps
innocents descending individually
one rung at a time
each with his or her back to us
(you cannot descend a narrow ladder
while facing the audience)
so we can see only the back
of each innocent as he or she
descends, a journey by its nature
self-effacing, and we, the audience, know
as he knows, as she knows
there is no turning back.
Yes, there is twisting and looking over
a shoulder, yes, even looking up briefly,
pointlessly looking up, pointlessly,
but no turning back from what waits
at the foot of the ladder.

ALICE KAVOUNAS

PETER MAXWELL DAVIES (b.1934)

Peter Maxwell Davies: 60
8 September 1994

There. the Rackwick boats
Are round Rora now
(See the patched sails, how
  They drink the wind!)

And the women count sixty
  boxes on the
  stones: haddock,
  cod, a huge
  halibut.

Summer's end: the patched
Fields of Rackwick
        Hold sixty stooks, in
  burnished ranks.
  No one in the valley
Will lack bread and porridge
  At the time of the first snow.

Orpheus in his cottage
  Near the crag edge
Ponders
The mystery of being and time; all
  His years a net
Of dancing numbers and notes.
  But sixty: this September
  All the birds of Hoy will sing blithely.

GEORGE MACKAY BROWN

ARVO PÄRT (b.1935)

Arvo Pärt in Concert, Durham Cathedral
November 1998

Sea-otters will be calving soon about the Farnes.

Perhaps you'll go there, in your coat, tonight.
Perhaps you'll go to Coldingham

or Lindisfarne, or, landlocked, wait, as if
you too were

sandstone: wounded, worn by wind, rain, light.

O Lord, enlighten my heart which evil desires have darkened

where the imperturbable pillars stand.

For you have fidgeted through sermons.

Hard to sit still with all your insufficiency about you, isn't it?

But you will listen through your permeable skin as if
this music were

slow wounding, swearing in, osmosis.

Ebba, abbess of Coldingham, will find her nuns forsaken, fidgeting,

but you, as Cuthbert, suffering for all, will make straight
for the sea, to stand all night
waist-deep in it,

in praise and prayer,

in fret, is it, or under the stars' bare
scattering of thorns –

O Lord, give me tears and remembrance of death, and contrition –

until dawn. When you will kneel down on the sand.
Sea-otters will come to warm you then.

But you must be as sandstone.

Make of this music an Inner Farne where you may stand alone.

For it *is* Farne, from Celtic *ferann*, meaning land,

where monks will dig a well for you of wild fresh water,
where you'll find not wheat but barley growing on bare ground,
where you will build a wall so high around
your oratory, you'll know the sky, it only
a while

as instrumental, wearing-in of wind and water. Listen

then, you'll find your own skin, salt, intact
as Cuthbert after centuries of wandering, still
permeable –

O Lord, forsake me not –

and one, as Arvo Pärt in his coat, will stand before
the orchestra, the choir, as if he too had only now
walked out of water

new, renewable, knowing the comfort of sea-otters.

GILLIAN ALLNUTT

EPILOGUE

New Music
To Larry Sitsky

Who can grasp for the first time
these notes hurled into empty space?
Suddenly a tormenting nerve
affronts the fellowship of cells.
Who can tell for the first time
if it is love or pain he feels,
violence or tenderness that calls
plain objects by outrageous names

and strikes new sound from the old names?
At the service of a human vision,
not symbols, but strange presences
defining a transparent void,
these notes beckon the mind to move
out of the smiling context of
what's known; and what can guide it is
neither wisdom nor power, but love.

Who but a fool would enter these
regions of being with no name?
Secure among their towering junk
the wise and powerful congregate
fitting old shapes to old ideas,
rocked by their classical harmonies
in living sleep. The beggars' stumps
bang on the stones. Nothing will change.

Unless, wakeful with questioning,
some mind beats on necessity,
and being unanswered learns to bear
emptiness like a wound that no
word but its own can mend; and finds
a new imperative to summon
a world out of unmeasured darkness
pierced by a brilliant nerve of sound.

GWEN HARWOOD

Klangfarbe

At the first performance
of his twenty-minute sonata
for trombone and lightbulb,

based – so the programme note told us –
on a reading of Jung's
Seelenprobleme der Gegenwart,

the most eloquent detail
and the one I shall remember
beyond all those whomps and rasps and splintered high notes

was the ping of the filament.

CHRISTOPHER REID

Tinnitus

August, sun beating the rooftops

for Alain Palacci

You are walking down a road that is white with dust.
It could be a dream; it could be the dream will last,
unlike any shape or shade of love you care
to name (or find and follow if you must).

Empty, white with dust, and something stopless in the air:
the chain-stitch of cicadas; a dynamo somewhere.

*

What if the music of the spheres
were the cryptic *ne plus ultra* of human fears ...

*

A single note drawn out
beyond imagining,
pitched for dog or rat
by a man with a single string
on a broken violin.

Easy to see that his penance
for gall is never to let
the music settle to silence.

*

Largo, allegro, con brio, glissando, crescendo,
vivace, veloce, da capo, da capo, da capo.

*

Something indelible behind your eyes:
the swift's wide wall-of-death between
the campanile of San Giovanni Battista
and balconies filled with flowers, a seamless scream
flowing behind the bird, a tiny twister
too sharp and shrill to be anything but lies.

DAVID HARSENT

A Music Sought

Shall I ever find
This music which I seek?
Both flutes and violins
Are scored within my mind
But something further off
I can just hear begins.
It takes both string and wind
And has to do with love

And all its thrill and drive,
Its landscape and its pace.
This music would preserve
Our best loves. They would thrive
And form a gracious dance,
Both keep our loves alive
And praise their circumstance.

Maybe no music can
Contain so deep a part
Of how we wish to live.
Both woman, child and man
Cry for the broken heart
To find a sound to give
A purpose to the hurt

We suffer and we cause.
Sometimes I hear the strings
Combine with flutes to sound
What is the best in us.
Listen, a music sings,
It's gone as soon as found,
Yet there's a universe

Which Bach and Beethoven knew,
Beethoven sometimes, and
Dowland often. There's
A starlight brilliance too
We but half-understand
Yet recognise as true –
The music of the spheres.

ELIZABETH JENNINGS

The Concert

for Peter Porter

The last piano in the world
Is about to be played
In a room empty of all other furniture.
There are parts of the floor you cannot stand on.
These parts are called 'holes'.

The pianist has the last clean white shirt,
The last hale suit with tails.
Some people won't believe
Our sponsors found a piece of soap
For him to wash his hands.
But he has no shoes.
Alas, there are no longer any shoes.

And the room fills with people,
Apart from those parts called 'holes' in the old language.
But some stand on the ground, in the 'holes',
With their heads looking over the floorboards,
Through ragged trousers, women's legs.

Latecomers sit outside in the long grass,
Among the foxgloves, thick vines of ivy
That strangle the plains, playing with
Stale, blanched bones of the unfortunate.

The old ones of the audience
Anticipate the works of Bach,
Mozart, Scriabin, Beethoven,
Debussy, Chopin, Liszt.

They are just names to them,
Names that make them think, or hum
What was written by someone else.

And the pianist sits down,
And the people remember to clap.
Then the old pianist weeps.
For all he can remember
Is *Three Blind Mice*.

DOUGLAS DUNN

The Other Great Composers

for Douglas Crase

They lived in places tourists don't care to visit
beside streams the obscure workings of local pride
insisted were rivers: there were willows or derelict mills
sometimes a boathouse with Palladian ambitions, –
in the backwoods, except that the towering pines were,
often as not, replaced by clusters of factory chimneys, –
isolate, the factories gone, the chimneys octagonal,
grand as columns remembering a Trajan victory
although severely unadorned. They lived in places where
commerce destroyed the Roman forts, the common fields
with red viaducts, canals now, like them, disused
and forgotten, depositories for ignorance, or else
they sank into the confines of a half-suburban dream
of pastoral they couldn't share: the works grew longer,
'unperformable' … The aggression of the ordinary,
the tepid love expressed in summerhouses too small
really to contain lover and beloved, the muted modes
and folksongs rediscovered, dead as elms, drove them
to new forms of learning and excess, ruthless
distortions of the academic tones and tomes,
chords that decayed over long bars into distances
where bell-hung, bird-haunted pagodas of their own
design rose up, tier on tier, to radiant mountains, –
mountains from which they confidently expected,
year after year, the arrival of the ancient and youthful
messenger who would confirm the truth of these visions.
It is impossible yet to say that they were wrong:
the music is unproved and undisproved; their operas
require cathedrals in which the angels and grotesques
come alive for one scene only; their fugues and toccatas
demand the emergence of a pianist eight-handed
like a Hindu god whose temples remain a sheaf of sketches,
whose religion is confined to a single head, maddened
or happy, dead-centred in a continent of neglect.

JOHN ASH

Knew the Master

You knew the Master. Come and talk about him
And we'll uncork a bottle, maybe two.
He used to write in bed in a red nightcap,
Or so the legend goes. And is it true
He played the harpsichord with both eyes shut?
Tell us about that scandalous affair
That set him working on the great quartets.
They say the Princess had a private stair.
You were his pupil and amanuensis –
You must have heard. What's that? You'd like to play
Some recent compositions of your own?
Well, not just now, perhaps some other day.

JAMES REEVES

Improvisation

In memory of Bernard Roberts, pianist, 1933–2013

A house of fantasy, a house of music
Grounded in time and built of trembling air,
A lofty many-sided School of Listening
Where players in the rooms above can hear
The music rising from the rooms below,
But those below hear nothing from above.
So, Bach, still counterpointing the foundation,
Is banned by a flight of years from hearing Mozart,
And Mozart, for all his gifts, stays locked behind
The singing pillars of his classic forms
As deaf to Beethoven's transcendent range
As Beethoven to Schubert, close yet far.
So Brahms, Schumann, Mendelssohn, Debussy
Soar up among the few still listened to,
While thousands in the cobwebbed catacombs,
Unheard, are spared the news that they're unheard.

Imagine the topmost floor of such a school.
His spirit could be part of the piano
He is playing, looking a little like Brahms,
Guiding his listening hands about the keyboard
As notes from the composers filter through him.
And though it's true not one of them can hear him,
You'd almost think that playing them, he *was* them.

A different view? Then let imagination
Build for the great musicians an academy,
A timeless concert hall, the sovereign source
Of pitch and harmony, to which their souls
Return as to a master class, where Beethoven,
His ears restored, advises on the *Waldstein*,
And J. S. Bach, delighted with his Steinway,
Improvises Preludes and Fugues, Book III.
And here – can't you see? – is a burly figure,
Listening attentively, making a few suggestions
As to modern fingering, seating himself
At last to perform a definitive
Prelude in C sharp minor from Book II –
Despite Professor Tovey's fervent muttering
And Wagner, amazed that a man from Manchester
Can play like a god despite his English tongue.

ANNE STEVENSON

Silence and Music

Silence, come first: I see a sleeping swan,
wings closed and drifting where the water leads,
a winter moon, a calm where wisdom dreams,
a hand outstretched to gather hollow reeds.

The four winds in their litanies can tell
all of earth's stories as they weep and cry;
the sea names all the treasures of her tides,
and birds rejoice between the earth and sky:

voices of grief and from the heart of joy,
so near to comprehension do we stand
that wind and sea and all of winged delight
lie in the octaves of man's voice and hand

and music wakes from silence as from sleep.

URSULA VAUGHAN WILLIAMS

COMPOSERS

These are not intended as a biographical resource, but should provide
some background to the music featured in the poetry.

ALLEGRI: Although it was forbidden to transcribe the setting composed for the Sistine Chapel, young Mozart famously memorised the *Miserere* at one hearing. It is memorable to ordinary mortals for its extraordinary high C.

BACH: Bach is by far the most popular with poets: the selection here refers to his cello suites, the choral 'Passions' and Mass in B minor (its 'Sanctus'), keyboard preludes and fugues and *The Goldberg Variations* (Warren Wilson has an entire book inspired by this). Heath-Stubbs reminds us that Bach was considered old-fashioned in his day (especially by his sons), but perhaps controversial too. For other poets he represents a kind of purity. Georg Erdmann (?1684–1737) was a school friend with whom in 1700 Bach travelled 180 miles (probably on foot) to Lüneburg to join the choir at the Michaelis monastery. Five years later, as John Gohorry explains, he set out 'from Arnstadt, where he was organist at the Bonifatiuskirche … to walk the 250 miles to Lübeck so that he could listen to Buxtehude (1637–1707), who was organist in the Marienkirche there.' Alistair Elliot's poem on Buxtehude deals with this visit. Line 12 of Gohorry's imaginary 'Journal' – which he has since expanded into a sequence including a cantata libretto – quotes Bach's own words. Charles Tomlinson takes the title of his poem from a piece by Arvo Pärt for harpsichord and strings.

BARBER: Best known for his *Adagio for Strings*, which was originally a string quartet movement but has been arranged for every imaginable ensemble.

BARTÓK: The *Concerto for Orchestra* remains one of the twentieth century's most popular orchestral showpieces (it includes a parody of Shostakovich). Fuller hears it as a brutal product of the war years (composed 1942–43, rev. 1945). *Duke Bluebeard's Castle* has held a particular significance for women poets; Helen Ivory draws on Bartók's one-act opera of that title. Szirtes, himself Hungarian, is remembering the composer's folk-song collecting, but knows that much more of the culture was also being 'collected' in his music.

BAX: He came from a talented family (brother to the poet Clifford Bax) and was himself the most extravagantly gifted man. Indeed, he even divided himself in two, adopting the alter ego of Dermot O'Byrne, a poet of the Celtic twilight. He once claimed that the poetry of Yeats meant more to him than 'all the music of the centuries'. The composer found his muse in the pianist Harriet Cohen, whose presence pervades this poem.

BEACH (née Cheney): One of a mighty handful of female composers to have achieved renown, though still not played much outside the USA. Scholes's note says it all.

BEETHOVEN: The *Hammerklavier* in Allnutt's poem is his phenomenally demanding late piano sonata, twenty-ninth of the thirty-two. R. S. Thomas would probably have been listening to Op. 27, No. 2 ('Moonlight'). Anne Stevenson was playing the third movement, introduction to the fugue, from the penultimate sonata, Op. 110. Alan Jenkins's sister's *Für Elise* is one of the *Bagatelles*. Beyond the piano sonatas and the symphonies, Beethoven composed much choral music (Matthew Arnold's response is worthy of the *Missa Solemnis*, but he had probably heard the composer's setting of Scott's 'March of the Monks of Bangor') and in his string quartets produced perhaps the most profound music of all: the six late quartets have long appealed to poets. Peter Redgrove recalled Ted Hughes playing them on their first meeting in Cambridge. Hughes's best-known response is to the almost unplayable *Grosse Fuge*. Here, a much later poem focuses on Op. 131 in the shadow of the suicide of his lover Assia Wevill. Beethoven was, of course, deaf and this irony has inevitably intrigued poets.

BERG: A highly influential composer of the 'Second Viennese School'. His violin concerto ('to the memory of an angel') was written following news of the death of Manon Gropius, who was Alma Mahler's daughter by her second marriage. 'Es ist genug' in Jones's poem means 'it is enough' and is the title of the Bach chorale that Berg quotes.

BERLIOZ: While the French composer was master of the High Romantic orchestral showpiece, he was also a very literary man, addicted to Shakespeare. His choral music transcends the 'revolutionary' image. Maxine Kumin writes about attending a rehearsal of the enormous *Grand Messe des Morts* under Boston Symphony's maestro, Seiji Ozawa.

BIRTWISTLE: *Minotaur*, to a libretto by the composer's regular collaborator, David Harsent – whose own work is featured here at the end of the anthology – was a considerable success at the Royal Opera House and was subsequently televised. Alice Kouvanas describes the stage action and makes no mention of music or composer, yet she recreates very powerfully the impact of that moment.

BRAHMS: Usually pitted against Wagner by the critics (hence the interest of Roy Fuller's poem, which is based on a photograph by von Eichholz), Brahms was an incomparable symphonist, a writer of vocal music (the 'Lullaby', the *Requiem*) and chamber music, but his piano works are equally important: an 'intermezzo' (which meant simply a short movement, here a piano piece) had originally been music between acts of an opera. Porter's poem is thus placed between Fuller, father and son. Brahms was in love with Clara Schumann, but had several infatuations: here for Hermine Spies, who ended up marrying a lawyer. John Fuller quotes the first of the Op. 105 songs inspired by Spies while in Thun in 1886, a work whose theme recurs in the Second Violin Sonata, also composed there. Marcia Menter's poem about his earlier sonata, Op. 78, was written for Roger Norrington's seventy-eighth birthday. If Fuller reminds us of Brahms's difficulties with women (and with his waistline), Penelope Shuttle gives us a very modern perspective. Her Queen Elizabeth Hall concert was conducted by Marin Alsop, one of the few well-known women conductors and an outstanding Brahms interpreter – here, of his final symphony with its extraordinary passacaglia finale. Shuttle is not alone in sensing the sexual charge that drives his work: unsurprising in a composer whose youth was spent playing the piano in brothels.

BRITTEN: Britten was very much a composer of place and the poems here show that it is possible to conjure the man simply through detail of the concert hall he built or the Suffolk town he made into a music festival. The town was Aldeburgh, where he settled with tenor Peter Pears; the concert hall was at Snape: 'The Maltings'. Alfred Corn concentrates on Coventry, the city of *War Requiem*, which incorporates the poetry of Owen. Britten was a pacifist, as well as a superb judge of poetry as can be seen in his song-cycles. All the poems here focus on the idea of a 'local habitation'. He forged a strong creative bond with Shostakovich; the Borodin Quartet, featured in Powell's poem, were Shostakovich specialists. Britten is presumably the absent 'maestro' in Crossley-Holland's poem: the clues are in words such as 'foundation' (the Britten-Pears Foundation?) and even a memory of his *A Midsummer Night's Dream* in those long ears (although the 'glagolitic' conjures another composer entirely). Ronald Duncan collaborated with him on *The Rape of Lucrece*. The trio behind 'Lament for Ben' is in fact from the third movement of Schubert's piano sonata D845 (formerly Op. 42). Schubert was always very important to Britten.

BRUCKNER: His granite-like, Wagnerian nine (or more) symphonies are the product not only of his experience as an organist, but of an intense and somewhat naive faith. The Eighth Symphony can last well over an hour and a quarter. As Porter reminds us, he was hijacked by the Nazis, but his music – including choral works – survived their interest.

BUTTERWORTH: A friend and contemporary of Vaughan Williams, influenced by folk song, master of the miniature (such as the one Motion mentions) and the song-cycle, he died at the Somme in 1916. Vaughan Williams's *A London Symphony* is dedicated to him.

BUXTEHUDE: The Danish composer's fame as an organist reached J. S. Bach, who walked 250 miles from Arnstadt to hear him, as related by John Gohorry. In Lübeck, Buxtehude had married the previous organist's daughter, as was apparently the convention. He himself had seven daughters, and Anna Margareta, the eldest, who speaks the poem, was indeed offered along with the post and turned down by Handel and Mattheson. Schieferdecker took the job and the daughter in 1707. Elliot notes: 'I imagine that as a young girl [Anna] heard the name of Orlando di Lasso, another organist and composer, and thought it was the name of an Italian poem, *Orlando Exhausted*, as it were. As Tony Harrison's son Max kept hearing the name Molière around the house, and piped up: 'I know that Molly Eyre. She's Jane Eyre's sister.'

BYRD: A Roman Catholic who survived the purges, because of friends in high places. Keyes's wartime poem is a double lament for a lost England. Byrd set (perhaps wrote) the lament for Tallis.

CAGE: Perhaps a blank page would have been the most apt representation of the Cage aesthetic in verse, but poets have been intrigued by both his ideas and the opportunity for puns in his name. Works such as the three Constructions deploy the junkyard of percussion described by Elliot but the 4'33" of silence has overshadowed everything else he produced, except his aphorism – equally apt under the circumstances: 'I have nothing to say and I am saying it and that is poetry as I need it.'

CHOPIN: The birthplace visited by Donald Davie is a manor house with parkland in Zelazowa Wola. Chopin came to London from France to escape the 1848 revolution and performed widely in Britain, though he was poor and very sick. In an epigraph to his poem, Philip Hobsbaum quotes a contemporary account describing how he was 'in the last stages of exhaustion', and how the dancers 'who went into the room where he played were but little in the humour to pay attention … His playing in such a place was a well-intentioned mistake.' Pleyel was a piano maker and composer.

COPLAND: The ballet *An Appalachian Spring* employs a Shaker hymn tune, *Simple Gifts* (sometimes known as 'Lord of the Dance'), alluded to by Richard Terrill.

COUPERIN: François was the most distinguished in a line of Couperins. The French Revolution already seems within sight by the end of Heath-Stubbs's Watteauesque poem. 'Mysterious barricades' alludes to a well-known harpsichord piece by the composer.

DEBUSSY: One of his piano *Preludes* conjures the sound of a drowned cathedral. There is a reference to *La Mer*, his celebrated 'symphonic sketches' (on which he worked in Eastbourne), near the end of Carol Rumens's poem.

DELIUS: Composer of exquisite landscape miniatures as well as larger choral works, Delius contracted syphilis (perhaps while managing an orange plantation in Florida) and from the 1920s came to rely on an amanuensis, Eric Fenby. Beecham is unrivalled as an interpreter of Delius. The poet Floyd Skloot has had more than his own share of ill health and there is a bond of sympathy within the poem.

DOWLAND: The greatest Elizabethan composer of lute music (briefly popularised in an album by Sting, and the inspiration for Rose Tremain's novel, *Music and Silence*), noted for his intense melancholy. He was a fine singer and may well have written the words to some of his songs too. A 'galliard' is a lively triple-time dance often set beside the slower 'pavane'.

DVOŘÁK: He is best known for the *Symphony No. 9: From the New World*, although the Seventh in D minor (which D. M. Thomas was hearing) is probably the greater work. The composer is also remembered here for a good-humoured salon piece as recorded by the popular violinist, Fritz

Kreisler. It too draws on folk song and it is said to have awakened the young Gershwin to the power of music.

ELGAR: The *Cello Concerto* was a late work, steeped in autumnal melancholy; his wife died shortly after its composition. Elgar's earlier setting of Newman's *The Dream of Gerontius* is an expression of his profound Catholic faith. The dying Gerontius's cry of 'Take me away ... is one of its most poignant moments. Of Gurney's poem, Philip Lancaster (his editor) writes: '"Beatitudes": probably the setting of the Beatitudes from Elgar's *Apostles*, first performed in the Gloucester Three Choirs Festival of 1904, in which Festival Gurney appeared as a soloist alongside Madame Albani at short notice (performance of *Elijah*). Both *Apostles* and *Dream of Gerontius* were performed at the Worcester Festival in 1905 and it would be that year's festival that Gurney is recalling.'

FAURÉ: Popular though the *Requiem* may be, it is his chamber music that is usually considered his greatest achievement. Charles Causley was presumably listening to one of the piano barcarolles; his words attempt to imitate the music. Floyd Skloot portrays him in the year of his death. The song in Penelope Shuttle's dream itself tells of a dream, the earthbound, benighted lover drawn to a heavenly image of the beloved.

FIELD: He toured Europe as a virtuoso pianist, composed seven piano concertos and did indeed invent the nocturne form, which Chopin took up.

FINZI: As Neil Powell reminds us, Finzi had a remarkable sensitivity to and understanding of poetry and was noted for his word-setting, particularly Hardy. He was also closely involved in the rehabilitation of Ivor Gurney. Nevertheless, the works most frequently heard today are his compositions for 'russet clarinet': the *Concerto* and the *Five Bagatelles*. A distinctly pastoral voice, he lived a rural idyll, but died as a result of chicken pox.

GIBBONS: Composer of the madrigal *The Silver Swan*. In Tennyson's day, his music was quite a rarity – as is a two-line poem by Tennyson. Hawthornden Castle is a writers' retreat and was the home of poet William Drummond, whose conversations with Ben Jonson about Shakespeare provide much of what we know about the greatest Elizabethan.

GLUCK: Mick Imlah equates Gluck's *Orfeo ed Euridice* with Shakespeare's unlucky play and uses it to illuminate the story of Kathleen Ferrier, who made the role of Euridice her own. Imlah's own tragically early death inevitably colours our reading of the poem. He is surely aware that 'Gluck' in German can mean 'fate'.

GRAINGER: Although John Gohorry doesn't name *Country Gardens*, instead quoting the words that have attached themselves to it, his poem is entirely in the spirit of Grainger's eccentric, exhilarating music, full of gusto and larks – not the ascending type – with a fair helping of the bizarre. It is also typical of Grainger to be a sparrow passing through the feasting hall of 'serious music'. Some jobbing musicians might consider the poem a very fair description of their life, too.

GRIEG: Nicholson, a lifelong Cumbrian, links the history of his own landscape with that of Grieg's Norway. *Solveig's Song* is one of the most melodic numbers from *Peer Gynt*.

GURNEY: Distinguished both as poet and composer, Gurney did not often set his own words. In 'Masterpiece' we have a unique example of a poet expressing what it feels like to compose and to know how little the world cares about such things. Gurney is fully aware of the irony in his 'Mere Quartett' and would certainly have regarded Beethoven's quartets as among western civilisation's masterpieces. Gurney had studied with Vaughan Williams but, after being gassed in the trenches, became increasingly unstable. N. S. Thompson writes that 'although he suffered a breakdown before the war, [he] survived the trenches but ended his days in a City of London mental hospital in Kent'. His musical reputation was rescued by Marion Scott and Gerald Finzi; his literary reputation established by P. J. Kavanagh, editor of his poems. N. S. Thompson, whose poem catches something of Gurney's own voice, is recalling perhaps Gurney's two poems with the same title, 'First Time In'.

HANDEL: German-born Händel was lured to London to write the opera, *Rinaldo* (1711), and that was the beginning of his love affair with the city, where he stayed for thirty-five years. The Aaron Hill referred to by Alison Brackenbury was the Drury Lane producer who staged the first performance. Handel wrote in all the genres of the time. The Op. 6 of Hill's poem is a set of 'Concerti Grossi', the equivalent of a Bach 'Brandenburg Concerto'. Giovanni Bononcini (1670–1747) was invited in 1720 to work at the new Royal Academy of Music, of which Handel was director; 1741 was the year of *Messiah*.

HAYDN: Based in Esterházy, Haydn wrote 104 symphonies in addition to quartets, masses and operas. No. 45 is the 'Farewell', because (prankster that he was) Haydn has the players gradually leave during the last movement. No. 99 in Scammell's poem is one of the 'London' symphonies, written at the time Holcroft published his homage: the imagery seems to refer to his oratorio *The Creation*, with its depiction of chaos, but that was a few years later.

HOLST: *The Perfect Fool* is ballet music, which should be as well known as *The Planets*. Interestingly, *Mars* (that mainstay of trench documentaries) was written a good while *before* the outbreak of the First World War.

JANÁČEK: He is highly regarded as a composer of vocal works which exploit the rhythms of the Czech language. Martyn Crucefix was listening to the song-cycle named in his title. Helen Ashley is thinking of his fifteen short pieces for piano, *On an Overgrown Path*, one of which is 'The barn owl has not flown away', commemorating the death of his daughter.

LIGETI: He began to be noticed after the Kubrick film, *2001, A Space Odyssey*, although no one in fact asked his permission to use the music. His biography makes grim reading. Aged three, in Hungarian-speaking Transylvania, he heard Romanian folk music, an alpenhorn player. Levin may be listening to his *Romanian Concerto*, forbidden performance in 1951 Budapest, although it sounds like later, darker Ligeti.

LISZT: A virtuoso and superstar, his compositions often misconstrued as merely 'showy', but – as Fuller discovers through pianist Alfred Brendel, who has written extensively on the composer (see his essay, 'Liszt Misunderstood') – there is a depth of spirituality, as represented by the 'transcendental study' which Kröte's pupil is tackling in Gwen Harwood's satirical poem. Rather like Donne, the older Liszt renounced his philanderings and took minor orders, becoming 'Abbé Liszt' in Rome in 1865.

LUTOSŁAWSKI: From Warsaw, he was a prisoner of war but escaped and made a living as a café pianist in the 1940s. The most enduring of Poland's many post-war composers, he became a frequent visitor to Britain in his later years. The piece heard by David Scott sounds as though it may have been the commemorative *Grave* for cello from 1981.

MAHLER: Kinsella does not name Mahler, but the profile, mannerisms and style of music are recognisable. Although no recordings exist, he was a charismatic and sought-after conductor. Alma was his wife. *Das Lied von der Erde* ('The Song of the Earth') is in effect a late symphony, using songs based on Chinese poetry. It ends with the repeated word 'Ewig …' ('Eternally …') *Kindertotenlieder* ('Songs of the Death of Children') is a song-cycle from 1905. Longley doubtless has the Northern Irish 'Troubles' in mind.

MARTINŮ: Born in a bell tower, studied in Prague, went to Paris: a distinguished and idiosyncratic symphonist with strong French influences. Helen Ashley's poem seems to be a response to one of the violin or cello concertos or sonatas.

MAXWELL DAVIES: Until recently the Master of the Queen's Music, 'Max' (himself based in the Orkneys) forged a unique bond with the Orcadian poet, George Mackay Brown. He has set many of Brown's poems and here the favour is returned. Rackwick in Hoy has been an important location for Maxwell Davies: it features, for example, in the *Lullabye for Lucy* (again to words by Mackay Brown), which celebrates the first birth in Rackwick for thirty-two years).

MENDELSSOHN: Mendelssohn was a child prodigy and phenomenally gifted. Skloot's poem is set in the final year of the composer's life shortly after his sister Fanny had died, when he was a Victorian national treasure. There are echoes of his *Hebrides* overture, the 'Songs without Words' and the symphonies inspired by Scotland and Italy.

MESSIAEN: A deeply religious, mystical composer, obsessed with birdsong, which he reproduced in keyboard works. Known too for his *Quartet for the End of Time* and for an ensemble in a concentration camp, including the clarinet, which is John Mole's instrument.

MONTEVERDI: Robin Fulton Macpherson was listening that morning to the evening *Vespers*, composed in 1610 – before Monteverdi made his name at

St Mark's in Venice – for an intimate setting in Mantua. The joyful *'Magnificat anima'* finally dispels the more troubled Latin phrases that occur to the poet.

MOZART: For those who like Koechel 'ratings' (Michael Flanders's quip when introducing his version of the horn concerto rondo): K285a is a flute quartet and K595 the final piano concerto, begun in 1788. That was the year of both K533 (Sonata in F, *Allegro* and *Andante*) and K563 (*Divertimento* for string trio). Although Mozart wrote several E-flat symphonies, No. 39 seems to be the one Hardy is singing to: his words can just about be made to fit the music of the third movement, especially the three beats of 'Love lures life on'. Mozart seems to bring out the inner workings of relationships and to attract the dramatic monologue. Gregory Warren Wilson refers to the composer's dissatisfaction with the way he was treated when on tour, and quotes a letter to his father written in 1777 from Mannheim: 'No money, but a fine gold watch. At the moment ten carolins would have suited me better than the watch, which including the chains and the mottoes has been valued at twenty. What one needs on a journey is money; and, let me tell you, I now have five watches.' The billiards legend (see Sheenagh Pugh) has much truth in it and when I worked for Hans Keller he used to joke about how much time the master spent playing.

PAGANINI: A virtuoso violinist and composer; a considerable celebrity in his time.

PÄRT: Estonian composer of hauntingly mysterious and often deeply spiritual pieces, including an elegy for Britten. He developed a distinctive 'tintinnabuli' style.

POULENC: One of *Les Six*, Parisian composer of playful and (later) deeply spiritual work in a wide range of genres. The woodwind sonatas and choral music are highly regarded.

PROKOFIEV: He has not inspired many writers, but he features as a card-player in Stewart Conn's Poulenc poem and Gareth Reeves puts him in a verse psychodrama voiced by Shostakovich ('D S C H'). While not so prominent in popular culture as the latter, Prokofiev wrote music that is known even by those who don't realise it: *Peter and the Wolf* for example, not to mention the theme to TV's *The Apprentice*. Osip Mandelstam's satire on Stalin (who was the likely model for 'the Wolf') cost the poet his liberty and ultimately his life. Reeves's line about the weather quotes Shostakovich's response to his rival's outline for his Sixth Symphony.

PUCCINI: *Madam Butterfly* has a particular appeal for Americans such as Mary Jo Salter, perhaps because of Pinkerton and something allegorical in the plot.

PURCELL: Dryden's is the best of several elegies on Purcell, who set a number of his texts and wrote incidental music for his plays.

RACHMANINOV: The spelling varies, but the music never ceases to affect, nowhere more than in the clarinet solo that opens the slow movement of 'Rach 2' which so moves Richard Terrill. As Seymour-Smith recounts, the composer's first attempt at a symphony was a notorious humiliation. Poets tend to sympathise with the idea of underestimated genius. Rachmaninov settled in America after 1917, so it seems appropriate that one of the poems about him brings an American perspective. The pieces here refer not only to his pianistic skills (phenomenally large hands, fit for those concertos and preludes), but to less well-known pieces such as *The Isle of the Dead*, a tone poem after a painting by Böcklin. Seymour-Smith's 'adulterous tearooms' recall the use of the Second Concerto in David Lean's *Brief Encounter*.

RAMEAU: A celebrated harpsichordist and composer of operas or opera-ballets. Symons evokes the 1890s rather more than the early eighteenth century when Rameau lived.

RAVEL: He wrote his *Concerto for the Left Hand* for Paul Wittgenstein, who had lost an arm in the First World War. The composer himself suffered a head injury in a car accident in 1932, which led to the symptoms described by Skloot. Some commentators have made connections between Ravel's condition and the obsessive style of his *Bolero*.

RESPIGHI: His finest achievements were orchestral showpieces, and the 'Roman triptych', of which 'Pines' is one.

SAINT-SAËNS: He wrote tone poems such as *Omphale's Spinning-wheel* and operas such as *Samson and Delilah* (source of the aria to which Ruth Fainlight refers); also, satirically, *The Carnival of the Animals*.

SALIERI: We do know that the composer and Viennese court conductor disliked Mozart, but (despite Heath-Stubbs's poem and Peter Shaffer's *Amadeus*) the poisoning is probably apocryphal.

SATIE: Minimalist piano pieces are his calling card: strong on wit, peculiarly appealing to our times.

SCARLATTI: Bunting had the B minor fugato sonata (L.33/K.87) in mind when structuring his late masterpiece, the Northumberland-inspired *Brigg-flatts*. Usually played on harpsichord. A popular recording of Bunting's own reading included a performance of the piece. He was a Quaker, so understood the significance of silence.

SCHOENBERG: He invented twelve-tone music, and was fascinated by (and sometimes seriously in fear of) numbers. Jo Shapcott knows that poets too like such pattern-making and palimpsests, the challenge of 'what's difficult', although her title is wittily deflating in a very English manner.

SCHUBERT: He wrote many piano pieces known to beginners, but also deeply tragic works. These include the String Quartet in G, D.887, to which Christopher Reid alludes in his elegy (whose title is Schubertian, too), the quartet to which Stainer's surgeons listen, *Death and the Maiden* (D.810, based on one of his hundreds of *Lieder*) and the song-cycle, *Winterreise*. Elements of the Wilhelm Müller narrative are tracked in Clucas's poem, whose rhythm echoes the walking pace of the cycle's opening song. Bernard O'Donoghue recalls the pianist Mitsuku Uchida, noted for her interpretation of Schubert (the poet must have been reading at the Voice Box ('on the floor above') next to the Poetry Library at the Southbank Centre). *Frühlingsglaube* ('Faith in Spring') includes the quoted German: 'now everything, everything will change': particularly apt for 1945. The fact that he died so young (like Frances Cornford's son, the poet John) preoccupies those who write about Schubert and leads them in several cases to explore other premature deaths.

SCHUMANN: Both Robert and Clara were pianists and composers; their romantic story is well known. He tended to express his love in song: *Dichterliebe* ('a poet's love') is his glorious cycle of Heine settings. The *Fantasy* in C major Op. 17 dates from 1836. Schumann contracted syphilis and became increasingly unbalanced. Brian Biddle alludes to the piano work, *Carnaval*, as well as to the composer's infamous plunge into the Rhine at the height of his madness. The poet and musician Ivor Gurney clearly sympathised: much of his own poetry – fractured, yet compelling – was written in asylums.

SHOSTAKOVICH: He wrote his *Preludes and Fugues* in homage to Bach and Joanna Boulter's poem is part of a long sequence in response to these. 'That opera' is *Lady Macbeth of Mtsensk*, which so angered Stalin. The 'reply' Storey is thinking of is the composer's self-proclaimed 'reply to just criticism', the Fifth Symphony: an attempt to win back approval from the Soviet authorities after writing what *Pravda* called 'Chaos instead of Music'. He was under pressure to commemorate Soviet achievements and some of his works do, ostensibly; but there are many cryptic personal references. His Eighth (one of his greatest symphonies) has no programme, but Dooley captures the wartime circumstances precisely. In his elegy, Tomlinson makes reference to the Fifteenth, with its controversial quotations from Rossini and Wagner and its recurring 'chime' at the end. The composer's finest late achievements were his deeply autobiographical and allegorical string quartets, especially the Eighth. Tony Roberts understands the dark humour that is so characteristic of Shostakovich.

SIBELIUS: The Finnish composer was famously silent for the last three decades at his home among the trees in Järvenpää. The god of the forest seems to wait behind Allnutt's lines; that silence is between them. But the 1909 tone poem *Night-ride and Sunrise* is also evoked. Tony Roberts alludes to the earliest symphony, *Kullervo*, suppressed for many years. The Fourth is so bleak (following Sibelius's throat cancer) that it came to be known as the *barkbröd* symphony – birch bark used instead of bread in hard times. Menter's (and perhaps the world's) favourite, the Fifth, ends with the celebrated swan-wing, 'hammer of Thor' theme. *Luonnotar* is an extraordinary tone poem for soprano and orchestra. It tells of the creation of the world. It also brings a shiver, since while I was typing up Robin Fulton Macpherson's poem the music came on the radio. The work was premiered in Gloucester in 1913 (Ivor Gurney was not in attendance, but he later wrote a less than successful poem about Sibelius's one string quartet: 'Out of the North comes the true tale of their sorrows,' he writes: 'Master – it is saluted, this great thing half doubted,/This great thing …').

SMETANA: Best known for his opera *The Bartered Bride* and the Czech nationalistic tone poems of *Ma Vlast* ('My Homeland'), Smetana was as much

188

plagued by deafness as Beethoven. In his late string quartet, *From My Life*, the 'incessant E' (see Nigel Forde's poem) represents this tormenting tinnitus.

STRAUSS: Georg Solti may well have been conducting *Der Rosenkavalier*, but Porter gives few clues and his poem is more about opera in general. Strauss was fascinated by the relationship between words and music and all the poets here explore this. *Ein Heldenleben* ('A Hero's Life') is an autobiographical symphonic poem – one of the last outpourings of German tonal music before the 'Second Viennese School'. If Ivor Gurney is to be believed, the Gloucestershire regiment knew their music, even if their German leaves something to be desired. *Ein Heldenleben* in fact quotes his earlier tone poem *Death and Transfiguration*, the work to which Vernon Scannell is half listening (half reading the Oxford anthology) in the final months before his own death.

STRAVINSKY: The Diaghilev ballet *Petrushka* (about a puppet that comes to life) was written between *The Firebird* and *The Rite of Spring*. The *Rite* had a notorious opening night in 1913 and Sassoon is amused by the later audience's apparent obliviousness to the music's sexuality. He mocks too the shifting tastes of the chattering classes as ('Concert-Interpretation' is a kind of war poem) he had mocked their reactions to war. He did not, however, have to contend with a mobile phone as Simon Rattle and the Berlin Philharmonic did at a Prom during the notoriously difficult high bassoon opening: Rattle stopped the bassoonist and started again. Morgan's poem describes the funeral of Stravinsky in Venice, watched by Ezra Pound, who was also to be buried there (as indeed Diaghilev had been) the following year.

SULLIVAN: Sullivan always wanted to be more than 'just' the other half of an operetta team, yet his work with W. S. Gilbert (such as *The Mikado* (1884–85)) contains his finest inspirations. Blunden (who spent time in Japan and was fascinated by the culture) must be thinking of 'Brightly Dawns Our Wedding Day', a tribute to the Elizabethan madrigal tradition which would have attracted his ear for sweet artifice.

TALLIS: *Spem in Alium* is a motet for forty voices: 'I have never placed my hope in any other than thee …' (*Spem in alium nunquam habui praeter in te …*). Affectionately referred to as 'Spam in Aluminium'.

TCHAIKOVSKY: *Francesca da Rimini* (the work Richard Kell's butterfly experienced) is one of his symphonic poems, evoking the damned lovers whirling in the fires of Dante's hell. The 'Old Usher' (and Oliver Reynolds has himself been an usher at the Royal Opera House) has evidently been hearing a lot of *Swan Lake*, but surely also *The Nutcracker*. Bernard Haitink's Tchaikovsky is much admired; he is an opera specialist. Monica Mason is a former dancer and director of the Royal Ballet.

TIPPETT: Robin Fulton Macpherson's poem is inspired by the *Concerto for Double String Orchestra*. Tippett is pastoral-political, so it seems right that he falls between Finzi and Shostakovich. He was a conscientious objector and a Jungian: both of these feed the concerns of the oratorio to which Martyn Crucefix is listening, which sets (as was Tippett's wont) his own libretto and makes poignant use of spirituals.

VAUGHAN WILLIAMS: *The Lark Ascending* – itself a response to a poem by George Meredith – has even displaced his own Tallis *Fantasia* as the nation's most popular classical piece: a soaring violin solo recorded by Kennedy and an exaltation of other soloists. Unsurprising then that so many poets should be moved to return it to verse. For Matt Simpson it conjures the spirit of Rupert Brooke and Hardy: the latter's poems are quoted and echoed in the last lines of Simpson's first poem. But RVW's work is often much grittier, more dissonant. The war-torn Gurney studied with him, a fellow Gloucestershire artist. The year of this poem (1923), Gurney escaped his hospital to visit him, begging for help: indeed, the poem was probably part of his plan as RVW's address appears on the manuscript (he always insisted, mistakenly, on adding a 'W' to his name). Gurney alludes obliquely to his teacher's Shropshire song-cycle, *On Wenlock Edge*, and to the walking imagery of *Songs of Travel*. Vaughan Williams's first wife was an invalid; his relationship with and marriage in 1953 to Ursula Wood may account for the late creative blossoming. Vaughan Williams delighted in elegiac finales; perhaps the man Ursula writes of in her poem had heard the bleak and unrelenting last movement of the Sixth Symphony.

VERDI: The opera John Smith attended was *La Traviata*. Verdi's libretti were often politically provocative. He married a soprano and, when she died, stopped composing.

VIVALDI: Ruth Fainlight's note on her poem explains that the *Dixit Dominus* was identified as Vivaldi's in 2005 by Janice Stockigt of Melbourne University. Vivaldi taught the violin at a girls' orphanage in Venice.

WAGNER: It is surprising – or perhaps not – how many of the poetic responses to Wagner are sardonic or pointedly minimalist. Dannie Abse's is very much from the Jewish perspective; performances of his work are still controversial in Israel. Brunhild/Brünhilde is a Valkyrie, put in a ring of fire by Wotan to challenge any passing hero.

WARLOCK: The adopted name of Philip Heseltine, whose best-known work is the *Capriol Suite*. He is given a third name in this elegy by his close friend and Oxford contemporary, the war poet Robert Nichols.

WEBERN: Some of the shortest, most dense atonal music ever written, by one of the key 'Second Viennese School' composers – who did indeed die in this strange manner alluded to by all three poets.

WOLF: Known almost solely for his songs. Venereal disease destroyed him. In 1898 he tried to drown himself in the lake described by Storey.

POETS

DANNIE ABSE: 1923–2014. Welsh, Jewish doctor-poet and self-professed music enthusiast. He had piano lessons from 'Miss Crouch' (who features in one of his poems) but admitted he preferred to 'play football with a tennis ball rather than do those exercises'.

GILLIAN ALLNUTT: b.1949. Lives in Co. Durham, winner of a Cholmondeley and the Northern Rock Award for her increasingly minimalist work.

MATTHEW ARNOLD: 1822–88. Poet and cultural commentator.

JOHN ASH: b.1948 in Manchester, an experimental poet based for many years in Istanbul but has learnt from the New York School.

HELEN ASHLEY: b.1946. Based in South Devon, influenced by both landscape and music.

PATRICIA BEER: 1919–99. Devonshire poet born into the Plymouth Brethren, known for her sharp, understated, plainspoken verse.

MARTIN BELL: 1918–78. Post-Auden intellectual associated with 'The Group'. He worked for a while as an opera critic.

BRIAN BIDDLE: b.1935. A poet-scientist living in Luton, who says 'Apart from my family, the great loves of my life have been music and chemistry'.

EDMUND BLUNDEN: 1896–1974. Best known as a pastoral war poet, he spent much time in Japan, which is perhaps why *The Mikado* appealed to him. At Oxford, he sang a baritone solo in William Boyce's setting of Dryden's *Secular Masque* for the Merton Floats.

JOANNA BOULTER: b.1942. Studied Music at London University and came to attention in 2007 with her Forward Prize-shortlisted *Twenty-Four Preludes and Fugues on Dmitri Shostakovich*.

ALISON BRACKENBURY: b.1953 in Lincolnshire where she played the piano as a child. A prolific poet who frequently writes on music. One collection is titled *After Beethoven*.

GEORGE MACKAY BROWN: 1921–96. Inseparable from Orkney and on countless occasions the inspiration for the music of Peter Maxwell Davies.

BASIL BUNTING: 1900–85. Northumbrian poet who became a cult figure in the 1970s after the publication of his long poem *Briggflatts*, and who always emphasised the links between poetry and music.

WILLIAM BYRD: 1543–1623. Like other composers from Campion to Gurney, Byrd would write his own lyrics. He probably sang as one of the Children of the Chapel Royal under Tallis's direction.

JOHN BYROM: 1692–1763. Manchester poet, medic and inventor of shorthand. Best-known lyric is 'Christians Awake! Salute the happy morn!'

CHARLES CAUSLEY: 1917–2003. Cornishman, who received the Queen's Gold Medal. A keen pianist throughout his life; the piano still remains in his cottage in Launceston.

GILLIAN CLARKE: b.1937. The National Poet of Wales. She was poet in residence at the Bridgewater Hall, Manchester. She is also a sheep-farmer.

HUMPHREY CLUCAS: b.1941. He has been a member of several cathedral choirs including Westminster Abbey. A composer himself, his *Requiem* was performed in Canterbury Cathedral.

SAMUEL TAYLOR COLERIDGE: 1772–1834. Coleridge responded strongly to sounds, as in his 'The Aeolian Harp'.

STEWART CONN: b.1936. One of the many significant Scottish poets to emerge in the late twentieth century; writes frequently about music. His poems have been set by composer Alasdair Nicolson and performed by the LSO.

ALFRED CORN: b.1943 in USA. Author of a dozen books, in poetry, fiction and criticism. A music amateur, he has composed works for keyboard and chorus, performed on several occasions.

FRANCES CORNFORD: 1886–1960. Underrated as a poet and overshadowed by her son, John, who was killed in the Spanish Civil War.

ROBERT CRAWFORD: b.1959. Poet and professor in St Andrews. The title of his collection, *Full Volume*, suggests musical preoccupations; invariably they have a Scottish accent.

KEVIN CROSSLEY-HOLLAND: b.1941. A distinguished writer of folklore and children's fiction as well as poetry about East Anglia. As son of the composer/musicologist Peter Crossley-Holland, he grew up among musicians, including, he says, 'several of the songbirds' of the mid-century: Rubbra, Finzi, Ireland, Howells, 'and their father-figure, RVW'.

MARTYN CRUCEFIX: b.1956. Winner of several major awards, with particular interest in Rilke, often drawing on the classical repertoire to shape his poems (he once did this for the complete Sibelius symphonies).

DONALD DAVIE: 1922–95. This poet and influential critic from Yorkshire confesses in one poem to 'Having no ear …'. Yet he often seems to be reaching for music.

MICHAEL DONAGHY: 1954–2004. A New Yorker based in the UK until his sudden death shocked the poetry world. Remembered for his 'traditional Irish' musical performances (tin whistle, bodhran and flute) and his scriptless recitations.

MAURA DOOLEY: b.1957. Currently poet in residence at Jane Austen's house. She has worked in film and her work has been set to music, most recently for a Norwich Cathedral event.

JOHN DRYDEN: 1631–1700. Was much involved with the theatre and its music. His spelling and punctuation have been modernised here.

RONALD DUNCAN: 1914–82. Specialised in verse drama and wrote a libretto for Britten, with whom he had a close friendship. He knew Kathleen Ferrier.

DOUGLAS DUNN: b.1942. Librarian turned academic, the finest Scottish poet of his generation – a keen clarinettist.

ALISTAIR ELLIOT: b.1932 in Liverpool. Noted for his translations. His *Medea* was performed in the West End and Broadway.

RUTH FAINLIGHT: b.1931. A friend of Sylvia Plath. Married to the late Alan Sillitoe. Much preoccupied with music in her enormous *New & Collected Poems*. She has written three opera libretti.

NIGEL FORDE: b.1944. An actor, lecturer and well-known radio personality, who included a series of imaginary monologues for composers' wives in his collection *The Choir Outing*.

JOHN FULLER: b.1937. Emeritus Fellow of Magdalen College, Oxford. He has provided texts for composers Nicola LeFanu, Brian Kelly, Gabriel Jackson and Robin Holloway. He is a keen pianist and classical music is as important a topic for him as it was for his father …

ROY FULLER: 1912–91. His day-job was with the Woolwich Building Society. Very much a poet of the turntable and stylus, especially in the collections of his later years.

ROBIN FULTON MACPHERSON: b.1937 on Arran, now based in Norway. He has written extensively about a variety of composers but is best known as the translator of Nobel Prize-winner (and dedicated music lover) Tomas Tranströmer.

DANA GIOIA: b.1950. Californian, former business executive who stirred up the creative writing departments with his article 'Can Poetry Matter?' He studied music composition, has written two opera libretti and been a music critic. He has a fondness for Finzi.

JOHN GOHORRY: b.1943 and based in Letchworth. Married with seven adult children and twelve grandchildren, rivalling Bach about whom he has written extensively. Noted for work of epic scope, and the odd miniature. Anna Krause has set part of his Bach sequence as a cantata.

JOHN GREENING: b.1954 in London. He likes to think he is related to Elgar, whose mother was a Greening.

IVOR GURNEY: 1890–1937. Troubled Gloucestershire composer and poet, whose work is only gradually emerging from the shadows of misprint and misunderstanding. Obsessed by, even possessed by, Schubert and Beethoven.

THOMAS HARDY: 1840–1928. He inherited his love of music (and a violin) from his father, who was an 'ardent' player for the church. The birthplace cottage was evidently a place of song and dance.

DAVID HARSENT: b.1942. He has won many international prizes (including the prestigious Griffin and T. S. Eliot) and has been Harrison Birtwistle's chief librettist since *Gawain*.

GWEN HARWOOD: 1920–95, Australian, studied and taught music (she was an organist) and collaborated with many composers.

JOHN HEATH-STUBBS: 1918–2006. His blindness began during Beethoven's *Missa Solemnis* when he was at Oxford. By then, he had abandoned the cello (resisting his musician mother) even though he was good enough to play the Bach suites. Later he would write a libretto for Peter Dickinson.

STUART HENSON: b.1954. A Huntingdonshire poet, teacher and winner of an Eric Gregory Award, whose best collection is *Ember Music*. He has produced and written several stage plays.

GEOFFREY HILL: b.1932. Oxford Professor of Poetry, internationally celebrated for his formidable poetry, its dark pastoral, its 'florid, grim music'. Influenced by Elizabethan composers, but his 2007 collection (which also features Brahms) took its title from his Handel poem. He is married to John Adams's librettist, Alice Goodman.

SELIMA HILL: b.1945, whose work can be both funny and surreal. Winner of a string of awards including Arvon, Forward and Cholmondeley.

PHILIP HOBSBAUM: 1932–2005. Academic, critic and presiding spirit of 'The Group', which fostered the careers of many more famous poets.

DAVID HOLBROOK: 1923–2011. Lawrentian poet of domestic affairs, but also a controversial cultural commentator, author of *Gustav Mahler and the Courage to Be*.

THOMAS HOLCROFT: 1745–1809. Son of a London shoemaker who became a playwright, novelist and occasional poet.

TED HUGHES: 1930–98. Deeply influenced by Beethoven, particularly the late quartets and the *Kreutzer Sonata*. The poem here is from a sequence written after the suicide of Assia Wevill. It appeared in an earlier version in *Capriccio* in 1990, in an edition of fifty copies.

MICK IMLAH: 1956–2009. Died of motor neurone disease, but not before the triumphant publication of *The Lost Leader*, an oblique account of Scottish history, from which this poem is taken.

HELEN IVORY. b.1969 in Luton. Her best-known collection is *Waiting for Bluebeard*.

ALAN JENKINS: b.1955. Surrey-born recipient of a Cholmondeley Award and Forward Prize-winner. Deputy Editor of the *TLS*.

ELIZABETH JENNINGS: 1926–2001. One of the few women poets recognised in the 1950s. Her Catholicism pervaded both her poetry and her appreciation of music.

PETER JONES: b.1929. Taught at Christ's Hospital. Edited the classic Penguin anthology of Imagist verse. He was one of the founders of Carcanet Press.

ALICE KAVOUNAS: b.1945 in New York to Greek parents; now living in Cornwall. She recently launched a location-based poetry app, 'Words in Air'.

RICHARD KELL: b.1927 in Cork. A keen music lover and for many years the *Guardian*'s poetry reviewer.

SIDNEY KEYES: 1922–43. One of the best of the Second World War poets and close friend of musicologist Hans Keller's wife, Milein Cosman. He was killed in action in Tunisia. Other poems of his are suggested by works of Schubert and Couperin.

THOMAS KINSELLA: b.1928. Often considered the most important Irish poet after Yeats, he spent much of his working life in the Irish Civil Service. As much influenced by traditional Irish music and song as by the serious classical composers. Seán Ó'Riada set him.

LOTTE KRAMER: b.1923. Came to England from Mainz in 1939 as part of the Kindertransport for refugees. Now living in Peterborough.

MAXINE KUMIN: 1925–2014. Popular American poet who emerged from the confessional school to become a popular chronicler of rural and family life.

GABRIEL LEVIN: b.1948 in France, brought up in the USA and based in Jerusalem since 1972. His interest in contemporary music often influences his poetry.

MAURICE LINDSAY: 1918–2009. A much anthologised poet in Scotland; a professional music critic for much of his life.

MICHAEL LONGLEY: b.1939 in Belfast. He received the Queen's Gold Medal for Poetry in 2001. He used to organise tours by Irish musicians. War and birdsong pervade his elegies.

NORMAN MacCAIG: 1910–96. He taught primary school children much of his life, but was a dedicated folk musician – he played the fiddle – and drinker of whisky.

JOHN MATTHIAS: b.1941 in Ohio and has lived in the UK. Composers are a recurrent topic; he admires Alfred Schnittke's belief in artists who 'have styles rather than a style'. His recent novel is *Different Kinds of Music*.

MARCIA MENTER: b.1953. The Brahms poem was a seventy-eighth birthday gift for the conductor Roger Norrington, whom she considers something of a 'Muse'. A writer and editor in New York, she 'studied singing at the Manhattan School of Music before realizing that her true vocation was listening'.

JOHN MOLE: b.1941. Poet, teacher, publisher and jazz clarinettist based in Hertfordshire.

EDWIN MORGAN: 1920–2010. Glasgow poet of astonishing fecundity and variety. He was the first Scottish 'Makar' (Poet Laureate) and has attracted the attention of composers, most strikingly the jazz saxophonist, Tommy Smith.

ANDREW MOTION: b.1952. The former British Poet Laureate has collaborated with, among others, the composer Sally Beamish, and has written a study of Constant Lambert and his family. 'Rhapsody' appears here for the first time.

FRANCES NAGLE: b.1946 in Nottingham, but settled near the Peak District. *Steeplechase Park* is her best collection.

ROBERT NICHOLS: 1893–1944. Known as a war poet, but was at Oxford with composer 'Peter Warlock', who introduced him to the world of music and musicians. He married Roger Quilter's niece.

NORMAN NICHOLSON: 1914–87. Once considered a major poet, now rather neglected; his love of poetry began with 'recitations' he gave at local events in Millom, in the Lake District, his lifelong home and the subject of most of his work.

DERMOT O'BYRNE: The pseudonym of the composer Arnold Bax.

CONOR O'CALLAGHAN: b.1968 in Co. Down. Among other awards, he received the Cloverdale Prize.

BERNARD O'DONOGHUE: b.1945 in Co. Cork. Widely celebrated for his understated poems about Irish rural life. A Medieval specialist at Wadham College Oxford.

PETER PORTER: 1929–2010. Australian-born, author of nineteen books and many reviews; famous for his erudition in all things poetical and musical (and for his record collection). Indeed, he claimed to value music (with regret) above poetry: 'I love music so much that, in poetry, I'm always looking for an authority in language that is not wholly dependent on meaning.'

NEIL POWELL: b.1948. Suffolk-based poet, critic and biographer of Roy Fuller, 'Amis and Son', George Crabbe and – most recently and not unrelatedly – Benjamin Britten. Music is central to his poetic output.

SHEENAGH PUGH: b.1950. Studied languages and has won the Bridport, Forward and Welsh Arts Council prizes for her work in over a dozen collections. She lives in Shetland.

PETER REDGROVE: 1932–2003. Winner of many prizes including the Queen's Gold Medal, he lived much of his life in Cornwall with Penelope Shuttle. His first encounter with Ted Hughes involved a late Beethoven quartet.

GARETH REEVES: b.1947. Based in Durham. His collection *Nuncle Music* is entirely about Shostakovich, an obsession which 'began with the string quartets' and with Volkov's *Testimony*. He is the son of …

JAMES REEVES: 1909–78. Teacher, lecturer, folklorist and prolific editor of anthologies, much influenced by Graves, who is, perhaps, behind 'the Master' in his poem.

CHRISTOPHER REID: b.1949. He won the Costa Prize for *A Scattering* (see his Schubert poem). Colin Matthews set his texts in *Airs and Ditties of No Man's Land*, and they were performed at the Proms by Ian Bostridge, Roderick Williams and the City of London Sinfonia.

OLIVER REYNOLDS: b.1957 in Cardiff. A versatile poet whose work is often theatrical. Like the speaker of his poem, he is an usher at the Royal Opera House.

TONY ROBERTS: b.1949 in Doncaster. Poet, critic, editor and former teacher of English, his work explores an impressive range of composers.

CAROL RUMENS: b.1944 in London. She studied the piano and intended to become a musician; her reputation advanced the cause for women poets in the 1980s. *Unplayed Music* won the Alice Hunt Bartlett Award.

MARY JO SALTER: b.1954 in Michigan, and associated with the American New Formalists. She has written a 'staged song cycle', *Rooms of Light*, for music composed by Fred Hersch.

FIONA SAMPSON: b.1968. Trained as a violinist at the Royal Academy, edited *Poetry Review*, and published an important book on contemporary poetry in addition to her own collections.

PETER SANSOM: b.1958. Director of 'The Poetry Business' and author of the invaluable *Writing Poems*.

SIEGFRIED SASSOON: 1886–1967. The most accessible of the war poets, he loved music although not as ardently as fox-hunting. Chiefly a satirist as we see in his Stravinsky poem.

ROBERT SAXTON: b.1952 in Nottingham. He won the Keats-Shelley Memorial Association's prize for his Elgar poem.

WILLIAM SCAMMELL: 1939–2000. A fiery satirist and pungent critic, he had a collector's passion for recorded music and would compare 'finds' in correspondence with the editor.

VERNON SCANNELL: 1922–2007. Once a boxer, but devoted his life to poetry (Heinemann Award for Literature, FRSL, Cholmondeley) and was a devout and knowledgeable music lover.

DAVID SCOTT: b.1947 in Cambridge. A 'parson-poet' in the tradition of George Herbert, he has witten libretti for the Children's Music Theatre.

MARTIN SEYMOUR-SMITH: 1928–98. Tireless biographer, critic and man of letters.

JO SHAPCOTT: b.1953. Multiple prize-winning poet, currently teaching at Royal Holloway. She has been set by Nigel Osborne, John Woolrich and Stephen Montague, whose *The Creatures Indoors* was premiered by the LSO.

PENELOPE SHUTTLE: b.1947. Celebrant of the mystical power of sexuality but much praised for her elegies to her late husband, Peter Redgrove, and a regular concert-goer.

MATT SIMPSON: 1936–2009. Much concerned with his home turf, around Merseyside, but he studied at Cambridge, like Vaughan Williams. Like Gurney, he found the composer a vital source of reassurance.

FLOYD SKLOOT: b.1947 in Brooklyn. Author of seventeen books; his first collection was called *Music Appreciation*, and he has paid especial attention to composers in their later years.

JOHN SMITH: b.1924. Literary agent and editor of *Poetry Review* in the 1960s.

GERARD SMYTH: b.1951. An Irish poet who was elected to the Aosdána in 2009.

MARGARET SPEAK: b.1942. A tutor in adult literature who lives in York.

PAULINE STAINER: b.1941. Related by marriage to the Victorian composer, John Stainer. Her potent and Emily Dickinsonian miniatures explore in particular the sexuality of the sacred.

ANNE STEVENSON: b.1933 in Cambridge. An amateur pianist from a musical family, although she has suffered much from deafness, which gives her 'Arioso Dolente' a particular power and authority. Known as Sylvia Plath's best biographer.

EDWARD STOREY: b.1930. A man of the Fens, about which he has written extensively, and founder member of the John Clare Society, he has provided five libretti for composers.

SEÁN STREET: b.1946. Actor, poet, broadcaster and academic with a particular interest in radio.

HAL SUMMERS: 1911–2005. A senior civil servant and author of several standard anthology pieces. Also played the piano and was a member of the London Bach Choir in his youth.

ARTHUR SYMONS: 1865–1945. Critic and Nineties poet who lived for a while with Yeats. The dedicatee of his poem about Rameau, Arnold Dolmetsch, was a pioneer of the early music movement.

GEORGE SZIRTES: b.1948 in Budapest, and came to the UK during the 1956 revolution. He has an understandable interest in the Hungarian composers (and has lectured on Bartók as part of the Southbank's festival, *The Rest is Noise*), although, as an artist himself, he is primarily a poet of the visual. 'Bartók' was written especially for *Accompanied Voices*.

NATHANIEL TARN: b.1928, American. A 'Penguin Modern Poet' in the 1960s and author of many volumes of poetry.

ALFRED, LORD TENNYSON, 1809–92. Tennyson has been a quarry for composers and here he returns the favour.

RICHARD TERRILL: b.1953. American poet and jazz musician, whose award-winning collection is tellingly titled *Coming Late to Rachmaninoff*.

D. M. THOMAS: b.1935. Known for his best-seller, *The White Hotel*, yet poetry has always been his metier, and music features repeatedly.

R. S. THOMAS: 1913–2000. One of the finest poets of the twentieth century, whose themes include faith, doubt and Welshness. As a vicar, he would have been closely involved with music of all kinds. In a poem about attending a Kreisler recital ('The Musician'), he notes, 'This player who so beautifully suffered/For each of us upon his instrument'.

N. S. THOMPSON: b.1950 in Manchester. A widely published poet and editor, he lives in Oxford, where he translates Italian fiction, and plays Renaissance music on the guitar.

ANTHONY THWAITE: b.1930. Distinguished, widely travelled editor (notably of Larkin), broadcaster, critic and academic, whose poems have been set by composers such as Jack Body and Christina Athinodorou.

TERENCE TILLER: 1916–87. A Cornishman, but forever linked to the Egypt of the Second World War. His 1979 collection contains a sequence of sonnets to different composers: 'Pictorial Calendar'.

CHARLES TOMLINSON: b.1927 in Stoke-on-Trent. A painter and professor, but above all a writer of international importance who plumbs the truths of music, in particular the modern masters to whom he returns obsessively.

URSULA VAUGHAN WILLIAMS: 1911–2007. In addition to her poetry, she wrote a biography of the composer, whom she married in 1953. She also wrote libretti for several other composers.

GREGORY WARREN WILSON: b.1956. Trained at the Royal Ballet School, studied composition at the RCM and is a professional violinist.

ROWAN WILLIAMS, b.1950 and Archbishop of Canterbury from 2002 to 2012. He is a distinguished translator of Welsh poet Waldo Williams. He lists as one of his hobbies 'playing the piano badly'.

ACKNOWLEDGEMENTS

Publication of this anthology has been made possible by a grant from the Ursula Vaughan Williams Trust, and by two private donations.

Extensive efforts have been made to trace the relevant copyright holders by letter and email. The editor and publishers regret any omissions, and apologise if any of the poems included have not been correctly attributed or if they lack the necessary permission or acknowledgement. In such cases they would be happy to be given further information.

The editor would like to thank those who have helped with the process of assembling this anthology over many years: in particular Richard Barber and Michael Middeke at Boydell & Brewer, but also Stephen Stuart-Smith of Enitharmon who was in at the beginning. Thanks especially to those experienced editors who gave their advice: Neil Astley, Kevin Crossley-Holland, Dana Gioia, John Lucas, Neil Powell and Michael Schmidt. For help with the final selection, thanks to Gay Edwards; and for proof-reading to Jane Greening.

Publisher and editor alike are grateful to the many literary estates, literary agents and small poetry presses (along with occasional larger ones) and to dozens of individual authors who were prepared to let their work be used for little or nothing. Above all, the team thank those who willingly offered poems or allowed poems to be used – and offer their apologies to those whose work did not make the cut.

DANNIE ABSE: 'The Maestro' from *Arcadia, One Mile*, Hutchinson, 1998, and 'Wagner' are reproduced by permission of United Agents (www. unitedagents.co.uk) on behalf of Dannie Abse. GILLIAN ALLNUTT: 'Arvo Pärt in Concert, Durham Cathedral, November 1998', 'Barclays Bank and Lake Baikal' from *How the Bicycle Shone, New & Selected Poems*, Bloodaxe, 2007, and 'Sibelius', from *indwelling*, Bloodaxe 2013, by permission of Bloodaxe Books. MATTHEW ARNOLD: 'Epilogue to Lessing's Laocoön' from *Poetical Works of Matthew Arnold*, Macmillan, 1890. JOHN ASH: 'The Other Great Composers', from *Disbelief*, Carcanet, 1987, by permission of Carcanet Press. HELEN ASHLEY: 'Frances Dancing with Martinů' and 'On a Farm Track, Northumberland' from *Ways of Saying*, Acumen, 2010, by permission of the author. PATRICIA BEER: 'Brunhild' from *Collected Poems*, Carcanet, 1988, by permission of Carcanet Press. MARTIN BELL: 'Verdi at Eighty' from *Complete Poems*, ed. Peter Porter, Bloodaxe, 1988, by permission of Bloodaxe Books and the estate of Martin Bell. BRIAN BIDDLE: 'Tone Row' by permission of the author. EDMUND BLUNDEN: 'A Quartet' from *Near and Far*, London, 1929, by permission of the Edmund Blunden estate.

JOANNA BOULTER: 'Prelude' from *Twenty-Four Preludes and Fugues on Dmitri Shostakovich*, Arc, 2006, by permission of the author and Arc Publications. ALISON BRACKENBURY: 'Yesterday Vivaldi visited me …' from *Selected Poems*, Carcanet, 1991, and 'Writing Rinaldo' by permission of the author and Carcanet Press. GEORGE MACKAY BROWN: 'Peter Maxwell Davies: 60' from *Collected Poems*, John Murray, 2005, by permission of Archie Bevan and the estate of G. M. Brown. BASIL BUNTING: lines from *Briggflatts*, Bloodaxe, 2009 by permission of Bloodaxe Books. WILLIAM BYRD: 'Ye Sacred Muses' from *Psalms, Sonets and Songs of Sadnes and Pietie*, 1588. JOHN BYROM: 'Epigram' from *A Collection of Epigrams*, 1727. CHARLES CAUSLEY: 'Fauré' from *Collected Poems, 1951–1992*, Macmillan, 1992, by permission of David Higham Associates. GILLIAN CLARKE: 'Erik Satie and the Blackbird' and 'The Piano' from *Making the Beds for the Dead*, Carcanet, 2004, by permission of Carcanet Press. HUMPHREY CLUCAS: 'Winterreise' from *Understanding Song*, Hippopotamus Press, 1991, by permission of Hippopotamus Press and the author. SAMUEL TAYLOR COLERIDGE: 'Lines to W.L.' from *The Poems of Samuel Taylor Coleridge*, Oxford, 1912. STEWART CONN: 'Playing Cards with Poulenc' from *The Breakfast Room*, Bloodaxe, 2010, by permission of Bloodaxe Books. ALFRED CORN: 'Coventry' from *Autobiographies*, Viking Penguin, 1992, by permission of the author. FRANCES CORNFORD: 'For M.S.: Singing Frühlingsglaube in 1945' from *Collected Poems*, Cresset Press, 1954 by permission of Enitharmon, agent to the Cornford Estate. ROBERT CRAWFORD: 'The Music Cleaner' from *The Tip of My Tongue*, Jonathan Cape, 2003. Reprinted by permission of the Random House Group Ltd. KEVIN CROSSLEY-HOLLAND: 'The Aldeburgh Band' from *The Language of Yes*, Enitharmon, 1996, by permission of Enitharmon Press and the author. MARTYN CRUCEFIX: 'Diary of One Who Disappeared' from *Hurt*, Enitharmon, 2010, 'Listening to Tippett Twice' by permission of the author and Enitharmon Press. DONALD DAVIE: 'In Chopin's Garden' from *Collected Poems*, Carcanet, 2002, by permission of Carcanet Press. MICHAEL DONAGHY: 'Cadenza' and 'Cage' from *Collected Poems*, Picador, 2009, by permission of Pan Macmillan. MAURA DOOLEY: 'The Lark Ascending' and '1943' from *Sound Barrier*, Bloodaxe, 2002, by permission of Bloodaxe Books. JOHN DRYDEN: 'An Ode on the Death of Mr Henry Purcell' from the first edition published in 1696. RONALD DUNCAN: 'Lament for Ben' from *Collected Poems*, Heinemann, 1981, by permission of the Ronald Duncan Foundation. DOUGLAS DUNN: 'The Concert' from *Love or Nothing*, Faber & Faber, 1974, 'Loch Music' from *St Kilda's Parliament*, Faber & Faber, 1981, by permission of United Agents and the author. ALISTAIR ELLIOT: 'Buxtehude's Daughter' and 'Exsultate Jubilate' from *Imaginary Lines*, Shoestring Press, 2012, and 'The Old Man comes out with an Opinion' by permission of the author and Shoestring Press. RUTH FAINLIGHT: 'Dixit Dominus' and 'Softly Awakes My Heart …' from *New & Collected Poems*, Bloodaxe, 2010, by permission of Bloodaxe Books. NIGEL FORDE: 'Kateřina Smetana' from *The Choir Outing*, Carcanet, 2010, by permission of Carcanet Press. JOHN FULLER: lines from 'Brahms in Thun' from *The Space of Joy*, Chatto, 2006, by permission of the author and Random House Group Ltd. ROY FULLER: 'On Hearing Bartók's Concerto for Orchestra' from *Collected Poems*, André Deutsch, 1962, 'Brahms Peruses the

Score of Siegfried' from *Buff*, André Deutsch, 1965, 'Benediction' from *Available for Dreams*, Collins-Harvill, 1989, by permission of the estate of Roy Fuller. ROBIN FULTON MACPHERSON: 'Morning Words', lines from 'The Cold Musician', and 'To an English Composer' from *A Northern Habitat, Collected Poems*, Marick Press, 2013, by permission of the author. DANA GIOIA: 'Lives of the Great Composers' from *Daily Horoscope*, Graywolf Press, 1986, by permission of the author. JOHN GOHORRY: 'Bach's Journal for George Erdmann' to appear in *Impromptus for George Erdmann*, Lapwing, 2015, 'Musicians Rehearsing al fresco' from *Talk Into Late Evening*, Peterloo Poets, 1992, 'A fiat for Joseph Haydn', by permission of the author. JOHN GREENING: 'The Lute at Hawthornden Castle' from *Knot*, Worple Press, 2013, 'American Music' and 'Field' from *To the War Poets*, Carcanet, 2013, 'Holst' from *Hunts*, Greenwich Exchange, 2009. IVOR GURNEY: 'Bach and the Sentry', 'Masterpiece' and 'Serenade' from *Collected Poems*, Carcanet, 2004, 'R. Schumann', 'To the City of Worcester' and 'To R. W. Vaughan Williams' from Philip Lancaster. Copyright rests with the Ivor Gurney Estate from whom permission has been gratefully received. THOMAS HARDY: 'Lines to a Movement in Mozart's E-Flat Symphony' from *Collected Poems*, ed. James Gibson, Macmillan, 1976. DAVID HARSENT: 'Tinnitus' by permission of the author in 2011. GWEN HARWOOD: 'A Music Lesson' and 'New Music' from *Collected Poems*, Oxford, 1991, by permission of the estate of Gwen Harwood and Penguin Australia. JOHN HEATH-STUBBS: 'Camille Saint-Saëns', 'Couperin at the Keyboard', 'Homage to J. S. Bach' and 'Mozart and Salieri' from *Collected Poems*, Carcanet, 1988, by permission of David Higham Associates. STUART HENSON: 'Harmonic', by permission of the author. GEOFFREY HILL: 'G. F. Handel, Opus 6' from *Broken Hierarchies*, Oxford, 2013, by permission of Penguin Books, Oxford University Press and the author. SELIMA HILL: 'Portrait of My Lover as Hildegard of Bingen' from *Portrait of My Lover as a Horse*, Bloodaxe, 2002, by permission of Bloodaxe Books. PHILIP HOBSBAUM: 'Chopin in London' from 'Study in a Minor Key', in *In Retreat and Other Poems*, Macmillan, 1967, by permission of the estate of Philip Hobsbaum. DAVID HOLBROOK: 'Dichterliebe' from *Selected Poems*, Anvil, 1980, by permission of Anvil Press and the estate of David Holbrook. THOMAS HOLCROFT: 'To Haydn' from *The Morning Chronicle*, 12 September 1794. TED HUGHES: 'Opus 131' from *Collected Poems*, Faber, 2003, by permission of Faber & Faber Ltd, Farrar, Straus and Giroux, LLC and the estate of Ted Hughes. MICK IMLAH: 'Scottish play' from *The Lost Leader*, Faber, 2008, by permission of Faber & Faber Ltd and the estate of Mick Imlah. HELEN IVORY: 'The King of Swords' by permission of the author. ALAN JENKINS: 'Für Elise' from *The Drift*, Chatto, 2000, by permission of the author and Random House Group Ltd. ELIZABETH JENNINGS: 'Mozart's Horn Concertos' and 'A Music Sought' from *Collected Poems*, Carcanet, 2012, by permission of David Higham Associates. PETER JONES: 'Alban Berg's Violin Concerto' from *The Garden End*, Carcanet, 1977, by permission of Carcanet Press. ALICE KAVOUNAS: 'After The Minotaur' from *Ornament of Asia*, Shearsman, 2013, by permission of Shearsman Books and the author. RICHARD KELL: 'The Butterfly Hears Tchaikovsky' from *Collected Poems*, Lagan Books, 2003, by permission of the author. SIDNEY KEYES: 'William Byrd' from *Collected Poems*, Routledge & Kegan Paul, 1988.

THOMAS KINSELLA: Lines from 'Her Vertical Smile' in *Collected Poems*, Carcanet, 2001, by permission of Carcanet Press. LOTTE KRAMER: 'Fugue' from *New and Collected Poems*, Rockingham, 2011, by permission of Rockingham Press and the author. MAXINE KUMIN: 'Rehearsing for the Final Reckoning in Boston' from *Connecting the Dots*, Norton, 1996, by permission of W. W. Norton and the author. GABRIEL LEVIN: 'After Webern' and 'Ground Offensive' from *To These Dark Steps*, Anvil, 2012, by permission of Anvil Press Poetry. MAURICE LINDSAY: 'Das Lied von der Erde' from *Poems 1940–1990*, Aberdeen University Press, 1990, by permission of the estate of Maurice Lindsay. MICHAEL LONGLEY: 'Kindertotenlieder' and 'Sycamore' from *Collected Poems*, Jonathan Cape, 2006, by permission of Random House Group Ltd and Wake Forest Press. NORMAN MacCAIG: 'Concerto' and 'Pibroch: The Harp Tree' from *The Poems of Norman MacCaig*, Polygon, 2005, by permission of Birlinn Ltd. JOHN MATTHIAS: 'A Note on Barber's Adagio' from *Collected Shorter Poems, Vol. 2*, Shearsman Books, 2011, by permission of the author and Shearsman Books. MARCIA MENTER: 'Schumann's Fantasy for Piano in C Major' and 'Sibelius's Fifth Symphony in the Dead of Winter' from *The Longing Machine*, Happenstance, 2007, and 'Sonata for Violin and Piano, Opus 78' by permission of the author. JOHN MOLE: 'Messiaen' from *Homing*, Secker & Warburg, 1987, by permission of the author. EDWIN MORGAN: 'Venice April 1971' from *Collected Poems*, Carcanet, 1996, by permission of Carcanet Press. ANDREW MOTION: 'Rhapsody' by permission of the author. FRANCES NAGLE: 'The Composer Amy Beach' from *Steeplechase Park*, Rockingham, 1996, by permission of Rockingham Press and of the author. ROBERT NICHOLS: 'Elegy for Philip Heseltine' from *Such Was My Singing*, Collins, 1942. NORMAN NICHOLSON: 'For the Grieg Centenary' from *Collected Poems*, Faber, 1994, by permission of David Higham Associates and the estate of the author. DERMOT O'BYRNE: 'A Girl's Music' from *Dermot O'Byrne: the Poems of Arnold Bax*, ed. Lewis Foreman, Thames Publishing, 1979, by permission of the Bax estate. CONOR O'CALLAGHAN: 'The Dream of Edward Elgar' from *The History of Rain*, Gallery, 1993, by permission of The Gallery Press. BERNARD O'DONOGHUE: 'Claire, Playing Schubert' from *Outliving*, Chatto & Windus, 2011. Reprinted by permission of The Random House Group Limited. PETER PORTER: 'A Brahms Intermezzo' and 'Covent Garden in the Sixties' from *Collected Poems*, Oxford University Press, 1999, by permission of the estate of the author and the agents Rogers, Coleridge & White Ltd; 'May, 1945' and 'The Pines of Rome' from *The Rest on the Flight*, Picador, 2010, by permission of Pan Macmillan and the estate of the author. NEIL POWELL: 'Borodins and Vodka' from *The Stones on Thorpeness Beach*, Carcanet, 1994, 'Finzi's Orchard' and 'Music' ('The Nature of Things') from *A Halfway House*, Carcanet, 2004, by permission of Carcanet Press and the author. SHEENAGH PUGH: 'Mozart Playing Billiards' from *Sing for the Taxman*, Seren, 1993, by permission of Seren Books and the author. PETER REDGROVE: 'Pianism' from *The Harper*, Cape, 2006, by permission of the estate of the author. GARETH REEVES: 'Sergei Prokofiev is dead' from *Nuncle Music*, Carcanet, 2013, by permission of Carcanet Press and the author. JAMES REEVES: 'Knew the Master' from *Collected Poems*, Heinemann, 1960, by permission of the estate of the author. CHRISTOPHER REID: 'Klangfarbe' from *In the*

Echoey Tunnel, Faber, 1991, by permission of the author and Faber & Faber Ltd; lines from 'The Unfinished' from *A Scattering*, Areté, 2009, by permission of the author and Areté Books. OLIVER REYNOLDS: 'The Composer's Ear-Trumpet' from *The Oslo Tram*, Faber, 1991, by permission of Faber & Faber Ltd and the author; 'Anton Bruckner: Motet for Men's Choir' from *Areté Magazine*, London, 2011, 'Old Usher' from *Hodge*, Areté Books, 2010, by permission of Areté Books and the author. TONY ROBERTS: 'After the Celibacy of Summer', 'Barkbröd' and 'Sausage' from *Outsiders*, Shoestring Press, 2014, and 'The Isle of the Dead', by permission of the author. CAROL RUMENS: 'The Submerged Cathedral' from *Poems 1968–2000*, Bloodaxe, 2004, by permission of the author. MARY JO SALTER: 'Libretto' from *A Phone Call to the Future*, Knopf, 2008, by permission of the author and Random House Inc. FIONA SAMPSON: 'Messiaen's Piano' from *Common Prayer*, Carcanet, 2007, by permission of Carcanet Press. PETER SANSOM: 'K563' from *Everything You've Heard is True*, Carcanet, 1990, by permission of Carcanet Press. SIEGFRIED SASSOON: 'Concert-Interpretation' from *Collected Poems*, Faber, 1961, by permission of Barbara Levy Literary Agency and the estate of the author. ROBERT SAXTON: 'The Nightingale Broadcasts' from *Manganese*, Carcanet, 2003, by permission of Carcanet Press. WILLIAM SCAMMELL: 'Small Fanfare for H. Robbins Landon' from *All Set to Fall Off the Edge of the World*, Flambard, 1998, 'A Touch of the Goldbergs' and lines from 'In the CD Shop' from *Black and White*, Flambard, 2002, by permission of Jan Scammell. VERNON SCANNELL: 'Indian Summer' from *Behind the Lines*, Shoestring, 2004, by permission of Shoestring Press. DAVID SCOTT: 'Playing Lutoslawski in Grasmere Church' from *Piecing Together*, Bloodaxe, 2005, by permission of Bloodaxe Books. MARTIN SEYMOUR-SMITH: 'Rachmaninov' from *Collected Poems*, 1943–1993, Greenwich Exchange, 2006, by permission of Greenwich Exchange and Aran Press. JO SHAPCOTT: 'Shapcott's Variation …' from *Of Mutability*, Faber, 2010, by permission of Faber & Faber Ltd. PENELOPE SHUTTLE: 'Après Un Rêve' and 'Concert, Southbank Centre' from *Redgrove's Wife*, Bloodaxe, 2006, by permission of the author. MATT SIMPSON: 'The Death Has Occurred …' and 'Vaughan Williams' Lark Ascending' from *An Elegy for the Galosherman*, Bloodaxe, 1990, reprinted in *Collected Poems*, Shoestring Press, 2011, by permission of Bloodaxe Books, Shoestring Press and the estate of Matt Simpson. FLOYD SKLOOT: 'Paganini and the Powers of Darkness' from *Music Appreciation*, Florida, 1994, by permission of the author; 'Delius & Fenby' and 'Ravel at Swim' from *Selected Poems*, Tupelo Press, 2008, and 'Mendelssohn at Thirty-Eight' by permission of the author; 'Fauré in Paris, 1924' by permission of the author and Eyewear Publishing. JOHN SMITH: 'Death at the Opera' from *Entering Rooms*, Chatto, 1973, by permission of Random House Group Ltd. GERARD SMYTH: 'Puccini' from *Daytime Sleeper*, Dedalus Press, 2002, and 'John Field' from *The Fullness of Time: New & Selected Poems*, Dedalus Press, 2010, by permission of the author. MARGARET SPEAK: 'Vivaldi's Bow' by permission of the author. PAULINE STAINER: 'Mrs John Dowland' and 'Music for Invasive Surgery' from *The Lady and the Hare*, Bloodaxe, 2003, by permission of Bloodaxe Books. ANNE STEVENSON: 'Arioso Dolente' and 'Kosovo Surprised by Mozart' from *Granny Scarecrow*, Bloodaxe, 2000, by permission of Bloodaxe Books; 'Improvisation' by permission of the

205

author. EDWARD STOREY: 'William Byrd's Virginal Music' from *Almost a Chime-Child*, Raven Books, 2010, 'A Postscript to Shostakovich's Reply' from *Last Train to Ely*, Rockingham Press, 1995, and 'Hugo Wolf at Traunkirchen' all by permission of Rockingham Press and the author. SEÁN STREET: 'K595 (Mozart)' from *Radio and Other Poems*, Rockingham Press, 1999, by permission öf Rockingham Press and the author. HAL SUMMERS: 'O Dowland, Old John Dowland' from *Smoke After Flame*, Dent, 1944, by permission of Dr Lucy Summers. ARTHUR SYMONS: 'On an Air of Rameau' from *Collected Poems*, Martin Secker, 1924. GEORGE SZIRTES: 'Beautiful Place' from 'Triptych for Music', in *An English Apocalypse*, Bloodaxe, 2001, and 'Bartók' by permission of the author. NATHANIEL TARN: 'For the Death of Anton Webern Particularly' by permission of the author. ALFRED, LORD TENNYSON: 'Orlando Gibbons' from *Poems and Plays*, Oxford University Press, 1965. RICHARD TERRILL: 'Appalachian Spring' and 'Coming Late to Rachmaninov' from *Coming Late to Rachmaninoff*, University of Tampa, 2003, by permission of the author. D. M. THOMAS: 'Music Student, First Violinist' from *Logan Stone*, Cape Goliard Press, 1971, by permission of the author. R. S. THOMAS: 'Sonata' from *Collected Poems*, Dent, 1993, by permission of the estate of the author. N. S. THOMPSON: 'Gurney: At the Front' and 'John Dowland on the Lute' by permission of the author. ANTHONY THWAITE: 'One of the Planets' from *Collected Poems*, Enitharmon, 2007, by permission of the author. TERENCE TILLER: 'Petrushka (Stravinsky)' from *That Singing Mesh*, Phoenix Living Poets, 1979, by permission of Random House Group Ltd. CHARLES TOMLINSON: 'If Bach had been a Beekeeper', 'Ode to Dmitri Shostakovich', 'Spem in Alium' and 'To a Christian Concerning Ivor Gurney', from *New Collected Poems*, Carcanet, 2009, by permission of Carcanet Press. URSULA VAUGHAN WILLIAMS: 'Silence and Music' and 'To the Man who Wanted a Symphony to Have a Happy Ending' from *The Complete Poems of Ursula Vaughan Williams*, Albion Music Ltd, 2003, by permission of the Ursula Vaughan Williams Trust. GREGORY WARREN WILSON: 'The Unsung Mechanisms' from *Jeopardy*, Enitharmon, 2003, by permission of Enitharmon Press; 'On Playing Ravel's Concerto for the Left Hand' by permission of the author. ROWAN WILLIAMS: 'Bach for the Cello' from *The Poems of Rowan Williams*, Perpetua, 2002, by permission of the author and Carcanet Press.

INDEX OF FIRST LINES

208

INDEX OF TITLES

212